Trench Knives and Mustard Gas

NUMBER SIX
C. A. Brannen Series

Trench Knives and Mustard Gas

With the 42nd Rainbow Division in France

Hugh S. Thompson

Edited, with an Introduction by Robert H. Ferrell

TEXAS A&M UNIVERSITY PRESS COLLEGE STATION

Library of Congress Cataloging-in-Publication Data

Thompson, Hugh S.
   Trench knives and mustard gas : with the 42nd Rainbow
Division in France / Hugh S. Thompson ; edited, with an
introduction by Robert H. Ferrell.—1st ed.
      p. cm.—(C. A. Brannen series ; no. 6)
   Includes bibliographical references and index.
   ISBN 1-58544-290-9 (cloth : alk. paper)
   1. Thompson, Hugh S. 2. World War, 1914–1918—Personal
narratives, American. 3. United States. Army. Infantry
Division, 42nd—Biography. 4. World War, 1914–1918—
Campaigns—France. I. Ferrell, Robert H.
II. Title. III. Series.
D570.342D.T49 2004
940.4 8173—dc22   2003019696

Contents

Illustrations

Acknowledgments

I am indebted, first of all, to Betty Bradbury for a most difficult task, namely, putting this manuscript on a word processor and thus enabling subsequent editing. The original memoir of Hugh S. Thompson had appeared in serial form in the *Chattanooga Times* of 1934, but the copy sent to the U.S. Army War College at Carlisle Barracks, Pennsylvania, was disfigured by blotches, presumably due to the aging of the originial, and by light places in the xeroxing that came from crinkling of the paper. It was thus necessary to resort to film. For all this it is impossible to thank Ms. Bradbury sufficiently.

In addition, many thanks are due Lt. Col. Edwin M. Perry, director of the U.S. Military History Institute at the War College; Richard J. Sommers, assistant director; David A. Keough, archivist; Richard Baker, interlibrary loan; and Cathy Olson, who persuaded a balky xerox machine to produce clearer copies.

Appreciation is also due to Suzette Raney and A. H. Mitchell of the Chattanooga-Hamilton County Bicentennial Library for information about the Thompson family; to Susan Curtis of the Darlington (South Carolina) Library for providing the name and address of Hugh Thompson, M.D., son of the author of this book; and to Dr. Thompson and his son, another Hugh, for their indispensable assistance and for sharing with me family photographs, papers, and many memories. Dr. Thompson's enthusiasm for the history of American participation in World War I and his knowledge of the subject made us immediate friends.

When I was teaching at the U.S. Military Academy at West Point a dozen and more years ago, Dr. Thompson had called, and at that time sent a copy of his father's memoir. His assistance in its publication with Texas A&M University Press has been wholehearted and utterly necessary, as was that of his son, who joined with enthusiasm in the details of the present book.

Thanks are also extended to John M. Hollingsworth, the skilled cartographer; to Mitchell Yockelson of the Modern Military Branch of the National Archives at College Park, Maryland, who found the U.S. Signal Corps photographs; to Kate Flaherty of the Still Pictures Branch, who made the prints for this book; and to the staff of Texas A&M University Press, who from the beginning saw the quality of *Trench Knives and Mustard Gas*.

—Robert H. Ferrell

Editor's Introduction

One of the most celebrated units sent to France during the United States' participation in World War I was the 42nd Division, or Rainbow Division. This famed organization was so named in 1917, following a proposal by (then) Major Douglas MacArthur to Secretary of War Newton D. Baker. The 42nd Division was, in fact, assembled from National Guard units from all over the United States. Its organization was a somewhat politically motivated initiative to assure wide national participation in the "War to end all wars." The name Rainbow caught the imagination of Secretary Baker, and it stuck. The 42nd became one of the four "veteran" U.S. divisions assembled in France soon after the American declaration of war in April, 1917. This was the Rainbow followed by Lt. Hugh S. Thompson, the author of this war memoir.

Thompson came from a well-known southern family. A great-uncle of his, Waddy Thompson, served in the United States Congress and was appointed Minister Plenipotentiary to Mexico prior to the Mexican War of 1846–48. His grandfather, another Hugh S. Thompson, commanded a battery in the firing on Fort Sumter at the outset of the American Civil War. He was influential in the Confederate war effort and was instrumental in ending federal occupation of South Carolina in 1876. He later served a term as that state's governor. And an uncle, another Waddy, wrote several history textbooks in widespread use in public schools. Thompson's father, Thomas C. Thompson, was mayor of Chattanooga during the Progressive Era.

Hugh S. Thompson was born in 1893 in Chattanooga and spent his boyhood there, developing a reputation as a student and athlete. He spent two years as a cadet at the Citadel, but left before graduating, upon the death of his mother in 1913. That year he accompanied his father on a trip to Germany. He was very impressed with the country and had no notion of the catastrophe to come, in which he would personally be pitted against those very same people.

Thompson sought service as soon as the United States declared war. Initially he planned to enlist in the Marine Corps, but he then secured an army commission in part through his father's influence, and in part based upon his military experience as a Citadel cadet and as a bugler in a Tennessee National Guard cavalry troop. After completing Officers Training School he was sent to France with the first contingent of casual (unassigned) officers and, to his great pleasure, was ordered to the Rainbow.

This book is a remarkable production. It is the only book Thompson ever wrote. The editor of the *Chattanooga Times,* in which it appeared in installments during 1934, described it as "a gripping story of the World War, written with personal directness and realistic touch approached by no other war writer." The present editor must agree with this appraisal. *Trench Knives and Mustard Gas* is hauntingly eloquent, and its scenes stay in the reader's mind. They seem to have been drawn yesterday. Much of the text's effectiveness lies in the change of Thompson's outlook as he moves through the account of his experience.

The Rainbow went into the line in Lorraine in early 1918, and it was one of the first Yank units to take over a sector of the Western front. While near Baccarat, Thompson was, for the first time, wounded and gassed. This was the first gas attack of the war directed against an American unit.

After its stint in the trenches of Lorraine the Rainbow was attached to the Fourth French Army in Champagne. As a part of that organization, the 42nd participated in the stalling of the last great German offensive, a series of "hammer blows" General Erich Ludendorff hurled at the Allied lines. General Ludendorff nearly succeeded. The casualties on both sides were heavy and gruesome. This last but ultimately failed German effort, the Champagne-Marne offensive, is considered by many to be the decisive turning point on the Western Front. Thompson was there and was wounded a second time in the ghastly German bombardment.

Thompson recovered from his Champagne wounds in time to rejoin his unit—I Company, of the 168th Infantry Regiment—in the first wave of the assault on the St. Mihiel salient in September of 1918. This was the first American planned and led offensive of the war. Although Thompson did not know it at the time, his younger brother was also in this battle, serving as a tank driver-mechanic. He was also wounded. For many months afterward, neither brother knew of the other's participation in the assault. It was at St. Mihiel that Thompson received his third, last, and most crippling wound, one that would dominate the remainder of his life.

After the St. Mihiel battle, Thompson's comrades were immediately thrown into the cauldron of the Argonne. Many did not survive. Thompson spent months on end in hospitals in France, undergoing several operations to save his leg. He returned to the United States to another round of hospitalizations and surgical procedures, long after the Rainbow made its triumphant homecoming to a ticker-tape parade along New York's Fifth Avenue.

Thompson never regained his health. He spent the remainder of his life with a painful limp, and he suffered frequent abscesses and difficulty in breathing as a result of the gas attack he survived. He received recognition for his service in the form of decorations and commendations. He was awarded the Silver Star, French Legion of Merit, and Purple Heart with three Oak Leaf Clusters.

After the war and his many hospitalizations, Thompson had difficulty settling into civilian life, as many veterans did. He moved through several jobs, finally establishing himself as a manager of insurance offices in Chattanooga and in Atlanta. He married Mary Ervin of Darlington, South Carolina, and the couple had a son. Later, at the outset of World War II, he sought to re-enter military service, believing he could make a contribution in a training capacity. But the U.S. Army had, perhaps, forgotten his gallantry and denied him the service he so much desired. He became, instead, a civil defense warden for the city of Atlanta until an abscess in his hip—one of many—again laid him low. On the advice of an orthopedic surgeon,

Thompson left Atlanta and moved to his wife's hometown of Darlington. There he engaged in trading horses and mules, an occupation he enjoyed immensely, until his wounds and the long-term effects of the gas on his lungs forced his withdrawal from gainful work. Thompson died of cancer in Darlington in 1961.

His son, who carries his name, wrote of his father the following:

> The war had been the central event of his life, and memories of it, as well as its physical aftermath, profoundly influenced the remainder of his life. His family and friends remember well, and all agree, that he had been marked, and was haunted for the rest of his life, as were so many millions, by that enormous catastrophe.

A Note on the Editing

Hugh S. Thompson wrote *Trench Knives and Mustard Gas* carefully, and his text needed little correction. The editor at the *Chattanooga Times* added chapter titles and occasional captions that I have removed and replaced with my own chapter titles. Thompson (it was in all likelihood he and not his editor) employed many exclamation marks, which, in retrospect, offered little to the narrative. These too have been removed.

Other editorial tasks have been slight: I used Arabic numerals rather than written-out numbers for regiments, such as in 165th Infantry; and for present-day readers of a much different generation I added explanatory notes as well as suggestions for further reading.

—Robert H. Ferrell

Trench Knives and Mustard Gas

Preface to the Original

I am incapable of analyzing my motives for having written this narrative of war, or more precisely, that part of a moving cyclorama that I saw firsthand. No doubt, the real reason is the presumptuous one of believing that the story may prove a valuable or at least an enlightening cross-section of America's brief but vital part in the cataclysm of 1914–18.

Whatever the motives, they have been fruitfully nourished by several relatives and friends, who think the story worth telling. These include the mother of a fallen comrade, whom I know only through correspondence and with whom I gained contact just three years ago. After a passage of letters, the mother asked that I try to picture for her the last two weeks of her son's life, a fortnight of poignant but precious fact not in her possession and the absence of which had left a spiritual void that had long cried out for filling. A crude, surging torrent of indelible recollections went forward in response to the mother's wishes. From that time she continued to urge a narrative of my entire experience as an infantryman in the American Expeditionary Forces.

I finally gathered together a few mementos in the form of old military orders, a sketchy diary kept during most of my active service, and a batch of letters saved by my family.

Grateful acknowledgment is also made for the aid of letters from fellow soldiers, a diary loaned by a fellow officer, and a conventional history of my regiment.

My chronicle is meant to be neither for nor against war. If it should aid the cause of peace, I would consider my past well worth the price—but I leave the preaching to more capable hands.

In this same spirit I have also endeavored to turn the story over to the "youth who was," rather than to the man of more mature reflection. A complete detachment is not possible.

After all, the two are one, inseparable. The youth drank deeply of war. The youth lived and breathed the life of a combat soldier. I hope that the older man intrudes only enough to make the youth and his comrades intelligible.

For reasons of propriety, fictitious names have been given to many of those who shared an unforgettable experience. On the other hand, these men themselves, both living and dead, would be the first to demand an integrity of personal impression. I have striven, therefore, for an honest picture, rather than for minute accuracy of irrelevant detail.

CHAPTER ONE

On the Way

The time was September, 1917. The place was a New York dock, overflowing with humanity. The transport *Kroonland,* with its cargo of newly commissioned reserve officers, made ready for sailing. Western Union boys scurried up and down the gangplank; swarms of relatives and friends crowded the "poop" deck, men awkwardly stolid and women tear-eyed. And all of this despite an ordered secrecy of departure.

Four of us, jammed against the stern rail near a gun crew of youthful sailors, complained bitterly of our shortsightedness. Tim, who was well knit and blondly handsome, had relatives in Manhattan who might have been there to wish us Godspeed. I had local kinspeople too. Why hadn't we thrown caution to the four winds, like some of the others?

Well, there was no use crying over spilled milk, we consoled each other. Boyhood friends, Tim and I soldiered together in the same squad at the Fort Oglethorpe training camp near our home in Chattanooga. We had bumped into the other two fellows during the monotonous line formations at Hoboken.

Sawyer, a big, good-natured shavetail with a pronounced "whataman" complex boasted frequently of his prowess on the gridiron. Walron or Barney, a trim, well-poised first lieutenant with a fuzzy mustache, seemed a bit older than our twenty-two and twenty-three years, owing to a more dignified bearing.

Now that we were really sailing, departure did not rest as lightly upon me as I had supposed. I became lost in a fit of reverie. Memories just a few days old and of the summer just passed tumbled over each other in a cascade of indelible pictures. There was the afternoon at Mineola; troops of the Rainbow Division had danced between rows of pyramid tents to the tune of rasping phonographs, with bright-eyed girls of all descriptions. And the enthralling evening on the Strand roof, where my cousin, Hugh, was a professional dancer. He was then awaiting orders to report for training to the Air Service.

Older memories drowned out those newer images: the ninety days of laughing, cursing, sweating labor to the tunes of "Tipperary," "Pack Up Your Troubles in Your Old Kit Bag," "Over There," and "Keep the Home Fires Burning"; the week-end leaves in the old home town, now swarming with men in khaki; the dates with the girl who wore my crossed rifles as a badge of understanding.[1] We had continued to talk of "when the war is over" and "when you come back," despite an epidemic of hurried marriages. Deep down, I realized that in face of such an intimacy with June I could never make a good soldier. The knowledge came home more vividly during our farewell meeting. Tim and I were to leave in the wee small hours. I had spent the early part of the evening with the family. All of us were to meet later in the depot café for the send-off.

June and I climbed to a favorite trysting place on Cameron Hill, above the city. Lights twinkled in the valley below us. The air was sweet with a faint odor of clover. We spoke the age-old endearments; we clasped in a long embrace—and I was sorry there was a war. An excursion boat drifted down the river, its lights making other lights in the water. Music and soft laughter came from the distant side-wheeler. These ceased, momentarily.

The revelers broke into plaintive song:

> *There's a long, long night of waiting*
> *Until my dreams all come true,*
> *'Til the day when I'll be going*
> *Down that long, long trail with you.*

The *Kroonland*'s whistle penetrated my dream world. The transport was moving. We waved hysterically to the bedlam of good-byes and dancing handkerchiefs. The crowded quay became smaller. A lump in my throat grew larger. Miss Liberty, her torch aloft, grew, shrank, and became a hazy lady. An impressionistic skyline did likewise. A scow with its burden of freight cars crossed our gentle wake. A hulking ferryboat followed. We glided through the Narrows and out into the open water.

Halifax harbor made a picture that might have been called "The Spirit of Transportation." Tugs, tramps, fishing smacks, a bevy of camouflaged transports surrounded the anchored *Kroonland.* There were schooners and lithe destroyers. Ships flew the emblem of the Red Cross. Black-hulled, red-bottomed fellows revealed massive sterns with "Belgian Relief" in great white letters.[2]

A pleasant rumor developed into reality. Shore leave in Halifax! Noisy figures ran over each other to climb down into waiting launches. We swarmed the quaint city—to the races, to the theater. It was a great day!

Detachments of threes and fours headed for the quay to be returned to the convoy. An undiplomatic native ridiculed a group with President Wilson's inept phrase, "Too proud to fight." "Uncle Sam—too proud, to fight." Fists flew in violent disagreement with Mr. Wilson.[3] Bobbies appeared to quell the miniature riot. Sawyer came out of the melee with a set of bruised knuckles. The dignified Barney returned with a "shiner" around his left eye from the fist of a Canadian soldier.

Our voyage was resumed the next day, after a bawling out from the commander of our party. We steamed through the tranquil waters. Women on a bluff high above the harbor wigwagged with semaphore flags: "Good-bye! Good luck! God bless you!" A train of red cars skirted the harbor edge in the distance. I imagined it was headed for New York and wished devoutly to be on it. We passed a British man o' war, whose band struck up "The Star-Spangled Banner." The twinge of homesickness was replaced by spinal chills as we snapped to salute.

We glided by red and black and green and gray-striped hulks, by an American tramp, whose motley crew returned our salutations. The crew went into a huddle against the starboard rail. Our waves splashed the tramp's bow as we heard the familiar refrain:

> Turn the dark cloud inside out
> 'Til the boys come home.

We struck Liverpool on a cold, foggy morning, after submarine scares, but little adventure. Cables home and a cursory sight-seeing accomplished, we made ready to move again. We fell in on the quay at dusk, five hundred strong. A captain commanded the party, first lieutenants leading company and platoon divisions.

Through gloomy, semilighted streets we hiked to our second-class carriages. There followed, with shades drawn for zeppelins, a trip broken only by a midnight repast at Oxford from the hands of comely Red Cross women.[4]

McLemore, a small dark fellow, and Van Zant, a medium-sized blond, shared our stuffy compartment. Sawyer entertained the newcomers with tales of his football prowess and with boastful prophecies of what he would do to the "krautheads" if we ever got to the front.

During a long busy day in Southampton, Tim and I managed a café reunion with other fellows from home—Ochs, Hood, and Saunders; Griscom, Brown, Grayson, and Lodor. Night fell upon another gloomy city and we hiked to a covered dock, seething with activity in a sepia glow of dim lamps. Sawyer went pop-eyed over a group of passing Scots, their kilts flapping and knees exposed to the raw night air.

Along with a bevy of British officers we boarded the good ship *Londonderry,* equipped for some three hundred passengers and now packed with upward of one thousand human sardines. The newly formed sextet shoved its way into a close engine room. Sawyer had words with a British officer and it took the best of us to avoid bloodshed. Our huge companion made blatant comparisons between American streetcars and the puny Southampton "dinkies"; references to crazy "lime juicers" who ran their cars on the wrong side of the street. "No, sir, gimme God's country!" The Britisher proclaimed that England was God's country as far as he was concerned and the battle was on. The good-natured Sawyer was soon apologetic. He offered the Britisher a swig from a newly acquired flask, with a whack on the back that nearly sent the smaller man sprawling. The Britisher recovered with the inquiry: "I say, do you have a glawse?" The battle was on again. It was forgotten as the channel steamer dived and passed through heavy weather. We were storm-bound! We struggled through masses of men to a drenched and overcrowded deck to overcome a creeping nausea. We stumbled over bending figures to a tilting rail. We answered an irrepressible call from nature, hanging on for dear life. Violent retching was universal.

The subdued crowd was disgorged at Havre on a raw, drizzling morning. Unkempt, woebegone troops disembarked from a nearby vessel. A British hospital train approached as we stood at ease in formation. All but the most shattered greeted us. On the whole, they seemed a happy lot, those bloody Tommys, on the way to Blighty.[5]

The Boulevard de François I was a riot of color when we quickstepped down its picturesque course. Small Belgians greeted us; French gobs in dark blue, red-tasseled caps and striped dickeys.[6] There were WAACS in crisp khaki, poilus in horizon blue.[7] Dirty urchins marched by our sides, gnawing cast-off food from docking transports.

"Vive l'Amérique!" shouted the foreigners.

"Cheerio, America!" the girls in khaki cried.

Down a hard highway we hiked, skirting the heaving channel. Up a punishing, winding hill to a windswept plain dotted with pyramid tents. A day was spent in sight-seeing. Back to camp, a freezing night followed on the bare tent floors, in full clothing and without other cover.

It was with few regrets that we retraced our steps next morning. We were again the center of all eyes at the railway station, in a scurry of bedrolls and moving orders.

The detachment clambered into second-class carriages. The

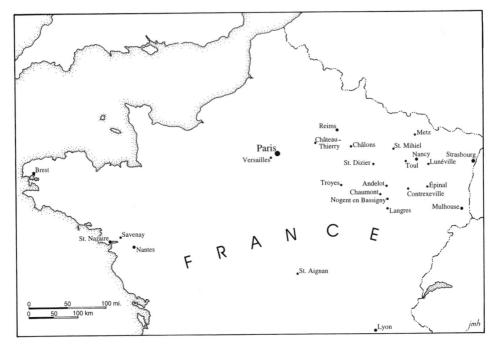

France. Map by John M. Hollingsworth.

six of us settled down in our home on wheels. We noted the ominous sign on the wall of our compartment. It was printed in several languages. "Do not talk. Be on your guard. Enemy ears are listening to you." Van poked "Frank Merriwell" in the ribs: "That makes it tough on you, Sawyer." A playful scuffle ensued. Mack griped with irritation. "Cut it out, you clowns. Get off my feet."

The train of tiny cars gathered motion, flat wheels beating a slow tattoo on the rails. We passed Evreux in due season and filled up with sandwiches at Versailles. We moved on again, headed for "somewhere in France."[8]

It was freezing when we descended from the cars at La Valbonne and hiked stiffly to the cold stone barracks of a French training school. Here the horizon blue of the poilu and his lilting "Madelon" immediately impressed itself as in colorful contrast to the khaki and "Over There" of a faraway Southern summer.[9]

One of the first men I ran across was "Moose" McCormick, the old Giant star. He had managed the ball team in Chattanooga four years before. I had worked out with the club that spring, a hero-worshiping kid who wanted to be a ball player. McCormick had broken the sad news that I would not do for Class A company. And now our paths crossed again, three thousand miles from the site of our earlier acquaintance.

The steep vineyards of the Rhône, with their dainty hillside dwellings, surrounded our bivouac. A great plain spread away to the northeast, over which the Jura and Savoy Alps, about one hundred miles distant, were visible on clear days. Their snow-capped peaks and rugged walls, bathed in sunshine, created the illusion of irregular piles of gold which one could hike to in short order.

We were formed into training companies, officered by battle-scarred Frenchmen who spoke English with varying degrees of fluency. Our company was particularly fortunate. Capt. Chautemps, a husky fellow, wore the dark blue of the Chasseurs.[10] A bushy beard was said to hide an ugly jaw wound. The captain immediately became "Camouflage" to all of our gang.

An intensive routine gathered speed, clear days alternating with flurries of snow. We started with a freezing reveille and early breakfast of war bread, confiture, "café au lait," and slabs of cold horse meat.[11] The mess hall, of heavy rafters and walls draped with banners of the past, might have been inherited from the time of Charlemagne.

A battalion of nondescript casual troops aided us with our training. Lithe Senegalese mingled with lighter complexioned Moroccans. There were Algerians and other colonials, a squad of Foreign Legionnaires in rusty blue with red piping, a Chinese, and an elderly Mississippian among them. "Camouflage" called this outfit "ze carneeval," owing to the gypsy-like riot of blues, reds, and yellows.

La Valbonne was rarely without an air of warlike realism. We practiced mock raids in an elaborate trench system with live bombs. Instructions followed with gas masks, chattering machine guns, Chauchat rifles, and booming trench mortars.[12]

Hikes to hillside villages, where we simulated the billeting of troops, and extended-order drills across country patterned after the formations used by "ze carneeval"—these were the things we learned from a band of proven warriors.

Off-duty events broke the busy schedule. We received stale mail from the States and home—home that began to seem as far away as Australia. A café near barracks was often filled with the officers of three armies. Clowns in barracks usually furnished sidelights of amusement. Akers and Johnson, two old sergeants, commissioned for the emergency, did much imbibing at an "out of bounds" estaminet.[13] Sometimes they would rouse the whole barracks with their zigzagging homecomings just before reveille.

Once they became lost on the cold dark plain. The pair split the night with platoon whistles. Questioning "toots" from the parade ground were followed by answering "toots" from other parts of the darkness. A series of "toots," nearer and nearer, and the confused pair had found each other. One of these men had soldiered at the army post near home. Perhaps that is how I fell in with them for several weekends in Lyons. I consumed quantities of champagne, in an effort to appear a sophisticated man of the world. Garcons rushed up and downstairs at the Hotel Continental in answer to the "old-timers'" wishes.[14] If the rest of us wanted a garcon for any purpose, the answer was usually delivered on the run, "Soree, m'sieur, ze lertna (lieutenant) Akeers, he call for ze champagne, toute de suite." A visit to the "Akeers" quarters found women competing strenuously for the favors of these lavish spenders.

It was the grizzled Johnson who thought up the best idea of all to get rid of his burdensome francs. With the aid of phrase books and the help of their feminine admirers, the old soldiers ransacked a Lyons shoe shop. Other femmes were invited from the streets. Fellow officers gathered to watch the pair give away feminine footwear, with sidesplitting speeches of presentation. It was here that I met Charlotte. My blood warm with champagne, I forgot all about a natural diffidence.

Back at La Valbonne, I now received French notes from the city, like some others. Spasms of conscience disturbed me considerably. It was exasperating, the way the images of June and the French girl would fight for supremacy, only to run together in an unintelligible blur of features.

Rumors filled the warlike air of La Valbonne! We were going to Russia. We were to be sent home to the States as instructors. We were to be parceled out among the British to take the places of highly expendable subalterns. One report had it that we were headed for new American divisions, just organized and landed.

The sextet vowed to try and stick together, at a hurried latrine consultation. Batches of "looeys" began to march away from the gray barracks.[15] Friends evaporated overnight. David and Spencer of our training camp company group, Grayson and Lodor from home, and many others went out of our lives forever.

There came the day. A gang of one hundred and thirty-odd, including the six of us, made ready for another pilgrimage to points unknown. We fell in with duffel bags, McCormick in command. I thought desperate thoughts about Charlotte. Was one always to be jerked away like this? She was to meet me in the Grande Theater Arcade on Saturday. How could I reach her?

I was hardly in tune with the leather-lunged marchers who changed trains in Lyons. They hiked through the oncoming dusk singing raucously:

> Glo-ree-us, glo-ree-us,
> One keg o' beer for th' four of us.

Dusk gave way to darkness. Anemic streetlights flickered around the Gare de Lyons.[16] A fit of melancholy seized me. Somewhere out there under that dim canopy of light was Charlotte. Melancholy was replaced by painful spasms of jealousy. Perhaps she was out there with another. There was no time, though, for much sentimental reverie, and I was snatched back to the realistic present as the irrepressible contingent piled into the cars still singing:

> Ma-de-lon, Ma-de-lon, Ma-de-lon!

CHAPTER TWO

Somewhere in France

A gripping, cramped-muscled crew descended from the cars at a bleak station. We had been two nights and a day on the hard benches of third-class carriages.

McCormick marched us to a square, abutting an ancient public building. He disappeared within. Rumors were rife about our location and what form of torture awaited us. Someone said we were in Vaucouleurs. Men hopped about and flapped arms to keep blood going. McCormick remained inside for a year. Snow fell and covered the square with a thin blanket. Passing onlookers made their way into their funny little white-roofed houses. An American caisson passed, making tracks in the snow. Horses, blowing steam from nostrils, were of ludicrously different sizes.

It was snowing hard now. The dull thumping of artillery beyond the old Hôtel de Ville seemed to fit into the wintry picture. McCormick returned to a growling contingent. Complaining ceased abruptly, as he was followed by a colonel, his adjutant, and a group of French lieutenants. The colonel announced crisply that we were at the headquarters of the 42nd Division, snowflakes settling on the speaker's cap and in the fleece of his trench coat collar. Only a few of the division's troops were in France at the moment. The rest were on the high seas and were due shortly.

The younger officer now stepped forward and read an order assigning our group of one hundred and thirty-odd to the Rainbow Division. He read another order assigning groups to the various infantry regiments. I listened with rabbit ears as names were read for the 165th, 166th, and 167th regiments. The adjutant barked the names in such rapid cadence that I could not be sure how the sextet had fared. I was petrified by a horrible, tense fear of separation. What if we had to part now? What if Tim and I lost each other?

The adjutant brushed the ominous sheet free of snowflakes. I set myself for a fourth agony of suspense. I inhaled deeply, then held it. The voice was barking again. "Pursuant to the authority contained in special order No. . . . the following named officers, Infantry Reserve corps, . . . will proceed to the headquarters, 168th Infantry. . . . First Lieutenant P. H. McLemore," I was startled. . . . "First Lieutenant Z. D. Setliffe, First Lieutenant A. H. Turk, First Lieutenant B. C. Walrof." I all but suffocated. . . . "Second Lieutenant J. R. Cullen, Second Lieutenant L. O. Irving, Second Lieutenant D. L. Preston, Second Lieutenant W. H. Sawyer, Second Lieutenant H. G. Smith, Second Lieutenant H. S. Thompson, Second Lieutenant C. S. Timothy." I heard no more. In a delirium of happiness, I even missed the names of Van Zant, Wallace, and Young that must have followed mine in rapid-fire order. "Whew!" I sighed, as Tim nudged me with his elbow. The colonel eyed us with irritation. There was an electric current of satisfaction from nearby files. Of the twenty-seven officers who reported to my regiment under this order and remained for active service, seven were killed in action and fourteen were wounded. Several of the latter were twice wounded and two of them were wounded three times.[1]

We were dismissed with orders to fall in again by regimental groups. Much backslapping accompanied a babel of congratulations. We fell in again happy. Barney was placed in command of our new group of thirty-odd. He marched us down the street for a meal in an estaminet. Finished, we climbed into waiting camions with bedrolls and two French lieutenants.[2] Similar groups did likewise. Wizened Annamites were in yellowish, drab, mounted drivers' seats.[5] We were off again, with a grinding of gears and a cloud of evil-smelling petroleum. White-roofed houses appeared and vanished. A billowy expanse of snow unfolded behind us as we skidded to one more "somewhere in France."

We came to a jerky halt, brakes squealing, and hopped into the snow-covered street of a tiny village. It had ceased snowing and the skies were clearer.

Lieut. Col. Townes, the officer to whom we were to report, was located in a spacious kitchen at the home of the "maire." The stern-looking colonel greeted us briskly. "I believe we shall get along together, gentlemen." He continued with a touch of sarcasm, "You young men will have to do most of the getting along, however."

My heart sank at this frigidity, recent happiness forgotten. Why had I ever wanted to be an officer? I visualized the troops who would soon be overrunning the village. These imaginary soldiers were decidedly unfriendly.

The colonel's voice brought me out of this painful abstraction. He had come over ahead of the regiment to prepare the area for its reception. With the aid of the French lieutenants, Garceneau and Claire, we were to pitch in and zone the town for billets. Our regiment was from Iowa, with "traditions." We would be expected to uphold them.

The colonel seemed to be addressing me personally, "It would not be a bad idea to rustle some mail from some source. The men will be hungry for word from home—and I'd hate to have my new officers chased through the snow with fixed bayonets." I wished fervently that I had never been sent to France.

The ensuing routine of verbal orders found us divided into pairs and trios. Some were to go to the headquarters and machine-gun companies. Others were to go to the first and second battalions. Ten of us were assigned to the third battalion in the following order: I company, Wallace and Young; K company, Turk and Timothy; L company, Walrof, Sawyer, and Thompson; M company, McLemore, Van Zant, and Cullen.

Tim and I did not even relish the separation that took us to twin companies. We decided, however, that we were perhaps better off. Alone, without a first lieutenant as a companion, one of us would be sure to catch the mischief.

We were searching for billets when the colonel approached and stated that a hurried change of orders was taking us elsewhere next morning. We were getting used to this jumping about without knowing where we were going.

Tim and Turk found a place for the night in a cozy cottage. A dainty parlor filled with bric-a-brac and quaint china; there were china dogs, china cats, china elephants. A china cat and her kittens rested upon a red plush pillow in a corner.

Barney, Sawyer, and I found a lodging in a rambling combination of barns and dwellings. Snow crunched underfoot as we entered a stone gateway. A horse labored upon an outmoded thresher in one of the stables. Old men and a boy flailed grain in another. The boy led us indoors. Out to supper in a dirty estaminet and the gang enjoyed the reunion. We returned to billets in darkness. A heavy thumping to the north was accompanied by carmine flashes like heat lightning. The spectacle of distant artillery got right down inside of me. How far away were the guns, I wondered? What kind of men were those way out there in the inky blackness? And the fellows who pulled the lanyards, were they angry at each other or did they just fire away without thinking of what happened later?

We spent the evening around a big log fire with an old man and woman. Lifelike reflections danced in shadowy corners and on the dark, massive rafters overhead. Drying peppers, or something like them, hung from the low ceiling. They were reminiscent of Tennessee's mountain cabins. A fit of homesickness tugged under my Sam Browne.[4]

Our bewhiskered old host explained in strange phrases that some celebrity of the War of 1870 had shared that very same fireplace. We were to sleep in the very same room, we gathered with difficulty.

"La guerre," droned the feeble old woman, "c'est terreeble, terreeble!"

Gray skies, icy streets, and a kaleidoscope of strange sights greeted us in the picture-book town of Rimaucourt. The

French lieutenants led us down a narrow street. A dingy church and an ancient Hôtel de Ville were hemmed in by rows of tan-colored houses of stone and mortar. A chateau stood opposite, with a walled-in park of firs and evergreens.

A battalion of Algerians marched past, machine-gun carts loaded with extra clothing, utensils of all sorts, and huge wine bottles in wicker cases.

An old fellow in a sky-blue smock marched up, beating a drum, with crowds of wooden-shoed natives following. Vapor came from excited throats, the drummer ceased with his sticks, and read from a dirty parchment. Finished, he tacked the paper on the wall of the Hôtel de Ville as the crowd babbled anew, pushing and shoving. Lieut. Garceneau explained that the town crier had read the names of all local youths called out in the 1918 class for conscription. The crowd dispersed, gesticulating; children clattered past with schoolbooks, their smocks flying in the December breeze, while an old priest, in cassock and funny flat derby, pruned a tree from a ladder top in the churchyard.

Col. Townes emerged from the chateau and ordered us to seek billets. A group was sent off to a neighboring village, where the second battalion was expected, and the rest of us scattered about in the small houses.

Sawyer found a place above a tobacco shop. A bell tinkled as a wizened little interpreter entered. The old lady who returned with him took one look at Sawyer's tough mug and protested, tear-eyed. The interpreter insisted. The woman dried her eyes with an apron hem and examined Sawyer furtively. "C'est la guerre," she finally shrugged, as the big fellow followed her indoors.

Barney and I were led down the bank of a creek that flowed from the chateau park and cut the street under a rustic stone bridge. Combination barns and dwellings lined both sides of the stream. Wooden shoes rested on nearly every low stone stoop, near frost-coated piles of manure.

Mme. Plantagenet greeted us hospitably in a small bakery and led us to a rear room overlooking a cold barnyard. A girl of about eleven and a boy of six hung about. The boy laughed a musical denial when Barney whacked his own back side in illustration and asked the youngster if his teacher ever spanked him. Hortense entertained us with a jargon that sounded like the lingo that American children call "dog Latin." Madame dragged Eugene into one of the bedrooms, while the boy's melodious protest said plainly, "Aw, mama, I wanta play with the soldiers."

We reported to the colonel in the Hôtel de Ville, to resume the billeting job which had been underway in the village we had left.

A stretch of cold plowed ground near a cemetery was chosen for a drill field. Natives were persuaded to double up their animals to make room in the barns for the incoming doughboys.[5] Pitchforks and crib-like wagons were busy transferring hay from loft to loft to prevent the prospective inhabitants from spoiling it for the livestock. Amid these scenes and activities I thought anxiously about the incoming soldiers. We turned in early after a busy day.

Sawyer appeared in the bakery next morning with his reluctant hostess of yesterday. He had assured us frequently that he was quite a man. Now he had proved himself a supersalesman. The stuttering "oui, oui" and "donnez-mois" that constituted his vocabulary had made the performance all the more remarkable. He put down the huge basket of vegetables he carried, while the old lady secured her big doughnuts of bread in exchange for dirty tickets. She chattered delightedly as a muscular arm reached out for the ring-like loaves. Sawyer picked up the basket and the strange pair departed, the overloaded soldier giving us a triumphant wink in passing. We followed them outside, convulsed. The toddling old lady and her bulky escort carried on like old friends. She chattered and gesticulated, tickled pink with her new friend. Her companion nodded with understanding, "Oui, oui, madame—sure, sure!"

Our crowd, now down to about twenty, trooped into the old church on Sunday. Children watched us with curiosity from behind clasped hands. Plain stations of the cross looked down from bilious walls upon an age-worn floor of flagstones and pews of ancient wood.

Evening brought the fearful news that troops were expected at an early hour on the morrow.

We turned in right after dinner. Barney was soon snoring, but I rolled and tossed, freezing underneath and perspiring on top, and finally dropped into a fitful world peopled with brown goblins, brandishing long, knife-like bayonets.

Rimaucourt was shrouded in cold, inky blackness when the interpreter roused us. The gang accumulated in the railway station. I could hardly distinguish the features of Tim and Barney, who huddled, shivering, beside me in the dim light of a lantern. Visions of the folks at home floated against a cloud of nervous cigarette smoke. I wondered if they thought of me. A pang of anguish went deep at the thought that none of those faraway friends could help me. I wondered if my companions were aware of my feelings or whether they secretly shared them. Col. Townes consulted a wrist watch; he gave a brusque command to follow him. A subdued crowd shuffled out under the black sky and groped for the invisible railway siding.

The dark train rolled in and came to a gentle halt. The engine panted contentedly as we stamped with cold feet on the crossties. A chorus of snores came from the "40 Hommes-8 Chevaux" boxcars.[6] Col. Townes went about looking for friends in the forward compartments. He climbed into a carriage near the engine. A stirring came from within, followed by muffled curses and sleepy greetings. A boxcar door squeaked. A brown figure, wisps of straw on his rough overcoat, descended in the cold dawn. He stretched with a grunt and was greeted with a series of questions from the gang.

"Where's company A?"

"Where's D?"

"Which way is the third battalion?"

An indifferent thumb jerked toward the end of the long train. We crunched off, looking for our companions. Squads climbed down sleepily and stacked arms along a cinder path between tracks. We located Capt. Clifton in a bedlam of baggage and brown confusion. Soldiers doused cigarettes and eyed us suspiciously. Barney saluted, "Sir, Lieuts. Walrof, Sawyer, and Thompson report for duty." The dark, handsome officer acknowledged the salute. Introductions to a group of officers followed, vapor coming from all throats. My own throat was clogged with the lump again. The strangers plied us with questions. How long had we been over? Had we been to the front? Was there any mail? What part of France were we in, anyway? Sawyer monopolized the conversation and Capt. Clifton surveyed him disapprovingly. A lieutenant who looked immaculate despite the long journey described the trip over with chattering teeth. The regiment had left on the transport *President Grant,* only to break down in mid-ocean. They had limped all the way back to the States and finally came over on the *Celtic.*

I mistook a small, rosy fellow for the bugler until Capt. Clifton addressed him familiarly. I realized with a shock that the juvenile was an officer. My spirits picked up. "If that kid can make good, I can," I assured myself. The fellow did not look over nineteen.

A slender, hard-looking lieutenant shoved his way into the group, sleep in his eyes, and hat tilted at a rakish angle. He seemed to be about thirty. A medium-sized, colorless fellow addressed him as Langworthy and asked how he was feeling. A rich baritone answered, "I couldn't climb no thorn tree with a wildcat under each arm!" The boy officer smothered a giggle. Lieut. Langworthy acknowledged introductions with poor grace, belched loudly, and left us.

A tall first sergeant appeared and announced that the company was ready for moving. Barney and Sawyer stayed behind to unload the kitchens while I led the company to billets. Troops were moving in all directions. I caught a comforting glimpse of Tim in passing. Early risers watched us from a cold sidewalk as we turned into the street assigned us. Men cursed when they climbed into the lofts of the chateau stables. Others complained upon entering an old barracks at the head of the street. Still others growled about the low bunks in stables opposite the chateau walls.

Officers followed me to a dingy wine-cellar room. Capt. Clifton complained about the billets. Why hadn't I secured better ones? I explained apologetically that they were all alike and that the street had been given us by Col. Townes. The captain would see that they were changed when things became more settled.

A company clerk set up a folding table and typewriter. The cocky Lieut. Langworthy cursed the billets, the orderly room, and the weather. It was with great relief that I led these unfriendly men to a large granary, selected for kitchens and officers' mess. A flagstone court swarmed with men rattling mess tins. Impatiently soldiers looked at me haughtily when we shoved our way to the somber interior. It was good to see Barney and Sawyer again.

Over a breakfast of hardtack, "goldfish," and strong coffee I placed the officers who sat about on supply and ammunition boxes.[7] The neat fellow was Scott. The colorless one, who seemed taciturn, was Malcolm. The boy officer was Jones, I learned, although the others called him Cherub. He proceeded to giggle at the repartee between a Cockney K.P. and grizzled mess sergeant.[8] Langworthy castigated an unknown noncom in a foghorn voice. Sergt. McDonough was going to catch hell if he didn't "get th' lead out of his pants."

The new confidence engendered by my first sight of Cherub evaporated upon the cold morning air. I told myself that I was in for some fire and brimstone, too. A day of unloading the troop train brought much coldness from Capt. Clifton and Langworthy. The hard day over, I piled into bed with Barney, bewildered. An overwhelming combination of homesickness, anxiety, and fear gnawed at the vitals of a badly scared "second looey."

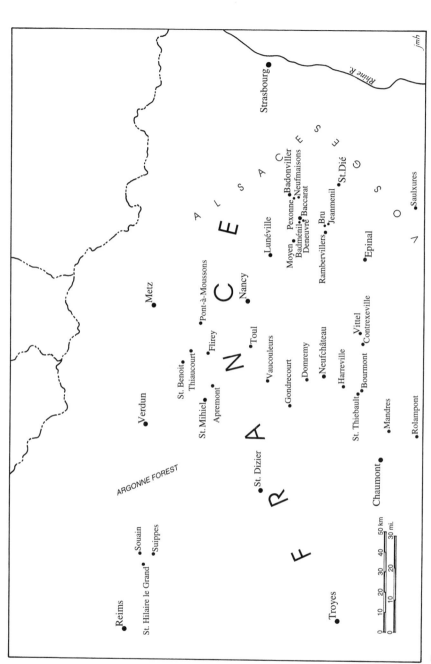

Eastern France. Map by John M. Hollingsworth.

CHAPTER THREE

Rimaucourt

Rimaucourt now swarmed with troops. The first and second battalions, the headquarters and supply companies, the band, and part of the sanitary detachment filled its barns and stables.[1]

The fire and brimstone expected after a discouraging start with this mob of Rainbow men came in the form of an oppressive hostility. Scott, Malcolm, and Cherub, fellow reservists, were not long in telling us that they had been treated as outsiders from their very first day at Mineola.[2] The verdict, "not wanted," hung over the cold, dark reveille formations in the chateau barnyard, over the job of manicuring Rimaucourt's streets with crude brooms and dead tree boughs. Matters were not helped when the men had to be cautioned against swiping wood from the natives. Capt. Clifton "passed the buck" to the new officers on this. A group of strange lieutenants talked to platoons of unknown men about stealing. "Squads east and west" on the freezing drill field brought a harsh opinion from the loudmouthed Langworthy. Most of the new officers "couldn't turn a platoon around in a ten-acre field." Our battalion commander seemed to like two things—cognac and cursing the helpless reservists. At officers' meetings Maj. Bronson smelled of rum and talked pompously about discipline.

A siege of snowstorms and zero weather prevailed. Deploying over stretches of white countryside to the tune of Maj.

Bronson's displeasure, everyone's mouth and ears were filled with fluffy ice at each squad rush toward imaginary Germans. Practice hikes down the slick roads brought an appropriate theme song for the new lieutenants' predicament. A song to an air like that of "Everybody Works but Father" informed us that the old officers were "real meennn":

> *Here is to Clifton, for Clifton he's a man,*
> *Here is to Clifton, on th' corner he will stand.*
> *Now Clifton, he's a daisy,*
> *He sets th' wide world crazy,*
> *Eins, zwei, drei, vier,*
> *Clifton's gonna buy th' beer—*
> *Here is to Clifton, he's a dam' fine man!*

The names of our group were conspicuously missing from chorus after chorus.

A regimental meeting in the Hôtel de Ville and Col. Lennert rebuked Levy, a Jewish reservist of the first battalion, for asking why the ill-equipped men could not wear knitted helmets, just arrived from the "mothers' clubs" in the faraway corn country.

A "zero day" brought mail for the two battalions. Officers censored an answering batch from the happy men. A letter described Barney as "a stuck-up guy from Noo Yawk." Another pictured me as "a red-faced hombre from somewheres below the Smith & Wesson line." "Ha, ha," added the writer, much pleased with his own brand of humor. My morale was given a body blow shortly after this incident. Sawyer was transferred— to the second battalion, leaving me in sole command of the fourth platoon.

Troubles for all came on with a rush. Epidemics. Scarlet fever, measles, diphtheria, mumps. Quite a few men were carted away to Neufchâteau and death before we had a chance to know them.

One fellow was tagged "Diphtheria" at the sanitary detail and placed in a loft by himself, where he was promptly forgotten. A day or so later he appeared in the granary mess line, flaming measles and all. Men dropped mess kits and made for nearby snowdrifts as Langworthy and Sergt. Kling gave the plagued one the devil from a safe distance. Hunger and isolation had overcome his fear of consequence.

Inspections revealed that the troops were in a terrible state. The feet of some were almost on the snow-covered ground. Others were without gloves or overcoats. Some wore light B.V.D.'s instead of winter underwear.

The few leisure hours usually found reservists in billets bemoaning the fate that had brought them to such an outfit. In this way I became acquainted with fellow lieutenants of K, L, and M, who had joined the regiment in the States. Knabe, of M, a Rhodes scholar, claimed that the hostile attitude was nothing but the result of "provincialism," whatever that was. Given reversed conditions we would probably have acted just as the home-town officers did, he argued. Needless to remark, our generous companion found himself in a minority of one. Albert, of I company, was a little older than the rest of us; his buddy, Hugh, seemed younger than Cherub. Talbot, of K, was a bit effeminate, I thought. Melvin, of the same company, looked nearly thirty and somewhat pompous.

Men began to register on my memory, as the wintry activities proceeded—Runyan, the disagreeable first sergeant; McDonough, my platoon sergeant, who seemed fairly decent; Owen, a youthful redhead; Dupree, a half-witted boy of eighteen; the six men of the platoon, who, with no gloves, left Springfields in billets and drilled with chapped hands stuffed in overcoat pockets; the poorly shod group, who wore the red hat cords of the artillery; the grimy Landers, of this crowd, whose Mongolian countenance had brought the nickname of "Chink." I learned piecemeal how the artillerymen had come to be in my army of fifty.[3] They had been on leave from Camp Mills when orders had come for the division to sail; and M.P.'s had routed them out of the roadhouses of Mineola. Hustled back to camp, they found their regiment quarantined with scarlet fever, so they were attached to L company, temporarily. Along with similar groups they were on the high seas before they had a chance to know what it was all about. Back at Mills again after the mid-ocean breakdown, they found their regiment had recovered and had already sailed for France, so they stuck with us.

Between freezing chores, Langworthy and Bonner, the latter a supply company lieutenant, attached to us for rations, "took the joy out of life." It developed that they hated Catholics. A Catholic myself, although not a devout one like Tim, I kept the fact quiet, gripped by the clammy hand of moral cowardice. This pair of roughnecks could find out for themselves that I was what they called a "knee bender," I decided.

More men crammed into my memory—Collard, a consumptive looking fellow, with a barking cough, believed firmly in the division tradition about a gorgeous rainbow. The band of color had appeared upon several auspicious occasions, it seemed. Beavers, a roly-poly corporal, was more skeptical. He hadn't seen "no rainbow before they left Camp Mills or out in th' ocean neither." Lawson and Bunce, my platoon guides, were surly and unfriendly. Jensen, a raw-boned Norwegian, and Stradikopulos gave my outfit a touch of universality. The latter dropped, in a decided accent, bits of his experiences as a lieutenant in the Greek Army. And the inseparable pair, McCarter and Stowers, who were forty and grizzled. Stowers, particularly, was a sight to behold. A narrow, alcoholic face stuck from the collar of an oversized coat, which swallowed the diminutive figure. Evidently, Stowers ran to baggy clothing. McCarter's description was perfect, "Looks like a family of possums moved out of the seat of his britches!" I had met the pair at summary court, where they were tried for drunk and A.W.O.L. Col. Townes sat at a desk in the Hôtel de Ville. I was called as a character witness. The trial over, I asked the colonel if I might return to duty. M.P.'s and prisoners guffawed and my ears burned with embarrassment as he eyed my forty-year-old charges and announced wryly, "Yes, you may go, lieutenant—and take your naughty boys with you."[4]

Cold, busy days passed in bleak monotony. We realized with a shock that Christmas had slipped up on us. Haute-Marne rested under a great white blanket. Rimaucourt was a veritable picture-book town. The chateau park, its firs and evergreens draped in white, might have been a scene on a Christmas card.

Scott was the only one of our group to receive mail, a stale plum pudding arriving early. Reservists were invited to a feast. A supply of cognac and rum was imported to Scott, Cherub, and Malcolm's attic billet. Tim, Turk, Melvin, and Talbot trooped over through a snowy night. Van, Mack, and Cullen soon followed. The pudding was saturated with brandy and set on fire. Our host's friendly face stood in bold relief behind the bluish flame. Huge chunks were cut with Melvin's Barlow.[5] The candlelit attic seemed brilliant after a few drinks of the fiery liquid. We drank to our French friends. We drank to each other. We drank to the next war and hoped there would be no Rainbow Division. Malcolm refused to drink and I thought him a "goody-goody." Cherub laughed and giggled as the supply of cognac ran low.

The party broke up. Galaxies overhead were swirling when the "goody-goody" Malcolm steered Barney and me to billets. A gang of soldiers reeled out of the corner estaminet. K company men in Madame's loft seemed to be hilarious, also. A far-away thumping penetrated my confused consciousness. We stumbled through the dark bakery and felt for the edge of our couch.

The day before Christmas dawned cold and clear. Thoughts of home were irrepressible; the absence of mail a tragedy.

There was to be a Christmas tree in the old church for the children of the village—Christmas á la Américain! Chaplain Roberts had scoured the country for toys. A tree was provided from the chateau park. The signal platoon had decorated it with a few colored lights. Officers and men packed the old edifice, with children by the hand. Barney and I had Hortense and Eugene. The church was brilliant with candles. The graceful tree sparkled near the altar of Mary. A piney smell mingled with a faint odor of incense. Our band occupied a front pew. Two Santas presided. One I recognized as the plump Levy, the Jewish officer from the first battalion. The other, I learned later, was a sergeant of Irish extraction.

The old padre appeared, said a brief prayer, and chanted a litany. In his native tongue he thanked the Americans for their generosity, his voice breaking with emotion. A linguist in our midst answered the priest in French.

Starry-eyed children went forward, received dolls, horns, and balloons, curtsied with shy "merci's," and returned to their soldier escorts. The band nearly took the roof off with "The Star-Spangled Banner" and "The Marseillaise." Outside in the snow, elders waited for their offspring. Tooting horns filled the night. We trudged through the snow with our French friends. Above the din, the band could be heard as it played a Christmas carol. A hush fell over the homegoers. Groups of French by the bridge sang softly, to the distant band's accompaniment:

A-des-te fi-delis.

Many turned out for midnight mass.

A late reveille followed on Christmas morning. There was a midday mess with the troops in the granary; scrawny turkeys and a few nuts were added to the usual rough menu. Hopper, the Cockney mess hand, kept men and officers amused with his comedy. The trouble with a turkey was, in his falling h's, too much for one man and not "henough" for two. Langworthy pantomimed with a basket, picking up the falling consonants, and the juvenile Cherub giggled and giggled.

Night brought a dinner with the Plantagenets. Father Plantagenet, a husky sergeant, was home on leave from Verdun. Hortense and Eugene gleefully displayed the simple toys found by their wooden shoes on Noel morning. Wine was brought out for visitors—Tim and Turk, Scott, Cherub, and Malcolm; the wounded soldier, who helped Madame with the bakery; the limping young postman, who held hands with Madame's kitchen maid, Mme. La Roque, a dumpy, middle-aged neighbor. A game of French origin was suggested by Mme. Plantagenet. Simple rules were explained in musical phrases, aided by significant gesticulations. A paddle wielder whacked the backsides of sundry blindfolded players. A correct guess as to who wielded the paddle and the guesser could indulge his or her sadistic tendencies. Mme. La Roque and Eugene seemed equally to delight in the fun. The old lady not only wielded a hefty paddle, she proved herself something of a stoic as well, during this game, which Cherub appropriately named "culottes chaud" or "hot pants."

The day after Christmas brought an issue of hobnail shoes from somewhere beyond our wall of isolation. While the welcome shoes were being issued in the granary, news came that an American outfit was marching through the village. It was snowing when we reached the chateau corner. Men on the cold sidewalks were laughing about a colonel, who had just passed, astride a small mule. The brown column followed, flowing like a river through the snowflaked street. An obvious weariness did not prevent a lot of banter. There was a volley of questions from the crowded sidewalks and answers from the passing column.

"What outfit, buddy?"

"Who wants to know? What's it to yuh? Ohio–Rainbow—166th Infantry."

"Where you headed?"

"Valley Forge," and shivering onlookers laughed raucously.

The river of brown continued; men were loaded with boxes, pillows, and utensils. A few carried rolls of toilet paper stuffed between pack tops and mess kit pockets. One fellow carried a mandolin and came in for much sidewalk kidding. There were exclamations from the shivering audience as groups struggled forward, worn-out shoes tied to packs and feet wrapped in rags and gunny sacking.

The column slowed down, buckled, and halted. A mule slipped and men worked with wagon and harness. Marchers dropped out, cursing wearily, "If th' old man 'ud get off that mule, he'd know what we wuz up against." Squads made for the low stoops, while a few lay down on their sides in the snow.

Barney and I spied McClung of our French training school detachment. He answered our questions from the chateau steps. His outfit had started from the Vaucouleurs area ten days earlier. Animals had arrived only a few days before the hike started and many were hardly broken to harness. There had not been enough serviceable shoes to go around and the troops had been in no shape for such an ordeal.

A bugle blew, men struggled to their feet with difficulty. McClung answered our parting question about destination, shrugging his shoulders, "God knows."

The column was underway again, but exhortations from officers and noncoms failed to rouse a scattered contingent that remained in the gutter snowdrifts. Some of these were taken into our billets and the afternoon spent rounding up the exhausted and chilblained. A few were whisked away by ambulance to the hospital in Neufchâtel.

When reveille sounded next morning, only a few troops turned out for the formation. The hobnails had frozen stiff in the night. Most of the men could not cram their feet into the new footwear. Groups scurried through the snow in stocking feet and made for the granary to thaw hobnails and icy "dogs." The problem was solved shortly; some buried their shoes in the hay, others slept with the hobnails on.

Events moved forward in rapid-fire order. I was delighted when Capt. Clifton, Langworthy, and most of the old officers were ordered to school at Gondrecourt. Many reservists departed also. Cherub went along, leaving Barney, Malcolm, and me with the company.

Details rolled in from the States with a bunch of wild mules. Foot soldiers laughed heartily as intrepid mule skinners were pitched into the snowdrifts near the drill field. A stubborn mule would sit on its haunches, a mule skinner tugging desperately at its bridle. Persuasion followed in picturesque language. It was not long before these same balky animals went away and came back meekly, dragging ration carts, supply wagons, and rolling kitchens.

Hikes started again in full equipment, wagons now accompanying troops down the slick roads. The old song glorifying the absent officers was sung frequently on the way out:

> *Maj. Bronson, he's a daisy,*
> *He sets th' wide world crazy.*

Chink, the lousy artilleryman, created a problem. Men who were no lilies themselves tried to get rid of him as a stablemate.

Barney moved him to a cold cellar. The idea became an inspiration. Men could be punished for minor infractions by being forced to share Chink's dungeon. In this way the grimy one made a great contribution to company discipline. We had a muster, the first payday since the troops had landed. Chink had to go without pay because Sergt. Runyan could not find his service record, so Barney, Malcolm, and I made up a pot for the unfortunate.

Grenades came in. A booming shook the stone wall near the drill field. Rifle grenades broke a succession of Springfields at the small of the stock. A few French rifles were secured. A day of instruction and Lieut. Claire galloped up on a horse to explain, with excited gestures, a mishap of the day before. One of our stray bullets had gone through a roof in a neighborhood hamlet and lodged itself in a housewife's kidney.

A batch of mail was devoured. Pleasure was dampened by fits of nostalgia. Sometimes one wondered if that faraway world had ever really existed. A note from the other Hugh in Issoudun apologized for making away with my Christmas box, received by mistake.[6] A card from Lawrence Hedges, a boyhood friend, announced that the writer was in the French ambulance service. "When are you coming over?" read the missive, which had gone all the way home and been forwarded back to France. One of my brothers had received his commission, another was trying to get into the Marines.

We were busy constructing a countryside trench system when Chaplain Roberts turned up with tragic news. Scott had been killed at Gondrecourt, in the midst of a mock trench raid, when a sack of grenades had exploded. The immaculate officer was a horribly mutilated corpse an instant later. Malcolm came over to live with us after the tragedy. That night when we turned in we rehashed the horrible details in the darkness. I could see Scott's friendly features outlined behind the blue flame of a Christmas pudding.

Rimaucourt was a bedlam of confusion—wagons, animals, and scurrying soldiers. Orders had come down from somewhere that we were to move. A regimental meeting and Col. Lennert assured us that there was to be no rotten march discipline like that displayed by our sister regiment. Officers were busy with demonstrations of proper pack rolling. We passed a final day of preparation and were off early.

The column filled the cold street. Mme. La Roque waved from the tobacco shop. The padre, shears in hand, climbed from a churchyard tree. We shuffled forward slowly, in fits and starts. Crowds lined the street, women with shawls to mouths. Malcolm and I, at the end of the company, found ourselves near the bridge. Groups of French left the sidewalks and mingled with the halted troops. Malcolm's old hostess appeared and he held one of her chapped hands awkwardly. I searched the crowd for the Plantagenets. There they were by the park gates. Madame leaned over the children and pointed. They clattered toward me. The mother called to Eugene to kiss me good-bye. The small boy dug a toe into the icy street, head down, and sniffling with a January cold. Hortense needed no prompting from "maman." I leaned over. She planted a wet, impulsive kiss on my lips. The column stirred with expectancy. The children clattered back to their mother. A command from across the bridge and hobnails hit the street in unison. The bugle blew, "Route step, march!" Wagons and equipment rattled. Soldiers waved to waving villagers. Waving villagers were dewy-eyed and vocal, "Bon chance! Bon chance!"[7]

The cold morning air nipped the ears. It irritated the lungs and nostrils. A chilly gust caressed the imprint of Hortense's kiss. It seemed that the little girl's mouth was still on mine as we crossed the bridge and stumbled up the slick hill into an uncharted future.

CHAPTER FOUR

The Raid

The column of two battalions clambered up the slick hill from Rimaucourt and made the neighboring village of Andelot. Our band met us and march music was the order of the hour. Singing followed. A hiker yelled "Let's go, gang!" and the gang responded:

> *Squads right, squads left, right front into line.*
> *Do it right, you son-uvv-a-gun, or you'll do it*
> *doubletime.*

K company, behind us, took up the burden:

> *Around her leg she wore a yellow garter,*
> *She wore it in th' springtime an' in th' month*
> *of May.*

I company joined the lilting chorus:

> *Far away . . . Far away,*
> *Oh, she wore it for her lover, who was far, far*
> *away.*

Bleak expanses of icy geography appeared and vanished in monotonous fields between villages. The enthusiasm subsided. Legs ached, pack straps cut into shoulders; unmercifully men fell out, exhausted.

Malcolm and I at the rear of the company fell behind to help stragglers into the overcrowded wagons. We inherited a pack apiece and several Springfields. Each rest period was used to catch up with the column. Sergt. Bethel and Corpl. Russell were dispatched to aid us.

More punishing hill and dale. More far-flung villages to bring false hopes of journey's end. More foot-weary stragglers. Morning passed. Afternoon waned. Men griped at each "fall in" bugle that brought them from the roadside drains to their blistered feet again. Everyone perked up at a plausible rumor. That distant steeple, high above the fading horizon, was the end. "By god, it better be." Men, officers, and animals were all but finished off by the steep climb into Nogent-le-Bas. Stomachs quivered with a nauseating weakness. Spots danced before the eyes. Villagers lined a dusk-laden square as we staggered to outskirt billets.

An advance detail supervised the billeting. Malcolm fell into a line of cold stables with two platoons. I reeled with two others into a dark schoolhouse. Packs were dumped into aisles between benches. A retreat formation was followed by slum and coffee.[1] Blistered feet were doctored and sprained arches taped by candlelight. Men groaned with pain and weariness. McCarter, as we hit the hay, began to reminisce about service in Mexico. "When we wus on th' border—" He was interrupted by Stowers: "Buddy, this ————— country you're in now ain't got no border." Men chuckled wearily and cursed their luck at the same time.[2]

We were up before day, to police the school and its evil-smelling latrine. Shafts of gray light revealed blackboards with pictures in colored chalk and partially erased sums in arithmetic. March order accomplished, platoon commanders pleaded with their men to stick it out—for the platoon, for the regiment, for the glory of the Rainbow.

We were on the road again. More bleak expanses. More far-flung clusters of barns and houses. We were on a treadmill.

Scenery was attached and was shoved behind by the excruciating process of "pickin' 'em up and putting 'em down."

We made Rolampont, somehow, where Gen. Liggett and
staff reviewed us from a freezing street corner.[3]

A series of wooded hills. An endless stretch of rolling country. A mule fell and broke a leg. The column obliqued around
the obstruction. A sergeant placed his "45" behind the mule's
jawbone. A muffled shot and the beast was out of its misery.

Outfits dropped off by companies M and L stumbled forward,
through the oncoming dusk. An invisible billeting detail greeted
us at a cluster of shadowy outlines. We collapsed into the billets
of Volsines. Rimaucourt lay sixty kilometers behind us.

Barney, Malcolm, and I came to an abandoned villa, whose
cold yard had long since grown up in winter weeds. Two platoons filled the building, while two others were housed in
barns around the corner. Hoary architecture lined two crossing quagmires of melting snow and mud. These led off over
stretches of farm land to the four points of the compass. The
wagons of peasants greeted us at reveille. Animals blinked in
dark stalls as the impatient mess line passed through a spacious stable. Rumor had it that we were near Langres.

Hectic activity followed a day of doctoring sore feet and
scraping off mud. An influx of gas masks, trench caps, helmets,
and automatic rifles came from the outside world. Battalion
maneuvers started, accompanied by a battalion of French.
Troops assembled between villages. Hillsides, held by imaginary Germans, were attacked across muddy fields. The make-
believe soldiers on the crests were replaced by doughboys,
who clicked triggers viciously and inquired with a drawl,
"Where you all from?" The answer, Iowa, brought the news
that the enemy were Alabamans, members of the other regiment of the 84th Brigade.[4]

The old officers returned from school, bringing the former
hostility with them. Langworthy was his old self as soon as
Barney and I refused an invitation to a drinking bout with a
group of noncoms. Knabe's generous verdict, "provincialism,"
did not relieve the oppressive burden.

I tried to figure it all out one night, in the darkness of our villa billet. Officers and two youthful orderlies snored in nearby bedrolls. The redheaded Owen "sawed gourds" beside me. Enemies and friends passed in review on the black wall. The unkempt Maj. Bronson did not know much, I assured myself, and tried to cover it up by bawling out others. "Better get some discipline himself," I mused, thinking of the cognac. Capts. Doss and Moore and Lieuts. Carter, Braddock, and Criss were deliberately offensive. My contact with them had been too slight for other judgments.

Capt. Allen, of K, reminded me of Sawyer. An old top sergeant, he was hard on the surface and friendly underneath. "Wish we had him for a captain," to the darkness.

And the cocky Langworthy. "The roughneck! Well, what do you expect from an ex-section boss on the Sante Fe Railroad? He's a dandy drill master," I admitted reluctantly. "If only he'd be friendly. All the same, I wouldn't mind having him around, if there's any dirty work to do at the front."

The next vision was that of the detestable Bonner, who had made life so miserable in far-off Rimaucourt. "Always horsing to get out of the supply company and into a combat outfit where he can see some action," I sneered in the shadows. "Hope somebody calls the little pimp's bluff."

"How about the reservists?" I asked my other self. There was a struggle to be fair. I was humbled by my own shortcomings. "Come to think of it, the rest are little better than I am." Turk, Tim, Wallace, Young, High and Smith, Setliffe, Preston, Irving, Van, Mack and Cullen trooped by in the shadows. "They're too young and inexperienced, like me," I decided, remembering that most of them were either in college or just out when America went into the big show.

Talbot was sort of girlish, even—and Sawyer had always been blowing. There couldn't be much bite where there was so much bark. Cherub had said he was a sophomore when he went to camp. If he had said he was a high school student I would have believed it. "Why he doesn't seem any older than Briggs and Owen—and don't know as much about military."

Knabe, the Rhodes scholar, was undoubtedly intelligent, but hardly fitted for a combat officer. The same was true of the goody-goody Malcolm.

Melvin was different. Nearly thirty, he had a dignified military bearing. "He's as strong a sister as Cherub and the gawky Cullen are weak ones."

And good old Barney, the pal who snored in an adjoining bedroll. "Well, I'll bank on that boy 'til the cows come home," I assured myself sleepily and snuggled up to the unconscious redhead beside me.

A bright sun had come and gone again, behind banks of gray clouds. Rumors filled the air once more. We were headed for the front, if latrine gossip could be relied upon. Abrupt orders were received in the midst of more maneuvers. Another bustle of wagons, men, and animals. We were getting used to this gypsy-like life. Bugles blew, officers barked commands, and the battalion assembled at Ormancey. A hard, swift hike took us to Rolampont and a waiting troop train. We piled into the "side-door pullmans." A night and a day brought us to the piling-out place of Moyen. A wet snow was falling as we hiked stiffly through the oncoming night toward the rumble of artillery. Silence and inky blackness enveloped the column. We left a hard highway and groped, single file, through the slushy streets of a hillside village. Men cursed impatiently when a billeting detail kept us waiting in ankle-deep mud. The thumping ahead continued. We floundered into the shadowy billets of Badmenil.

That Badmenil became "Mudville" in the vernacular of expressive doughboys was not the result of chance judgment. A wet snow continued to melt upon this obscure village in the department of Meurthe. It tumbled lazily upon our barnyard mess shack and in front of our dingy orderly room. It melted upon the stoops of billets, whose cellars were marked with Lorraine crosses, indicating places of refuge from air raids.[5] It floated down upon a system of ditches surrounding an old cemetery.

Troops formed with Springfields carried at trail or upon the toes of hobnails, to keep the rifles serviceable. Soldiers splashed about as though they had never known any other existence.

Langworthy, Malcolm, Cherub, and I, with Owen and Briggs, shared a small bare room across from Capt. Clifton and Barney. Our hostess, an untidy but motherly woman, made us welcome around her kitchen fire, mud and all. Hot bricks for cold feet greeted us when we piled into our bedrolls.

A breakfast mess brought all sorts of news. K company had rolled into town, after a week in Lunéville, unloading ammunition. Tim and I were together again. The K bunch dispensed the gossip. We were near Baccarat. Infantry units were already in trenches with the French, some twenty kilometers to the north. Our first battalion was among them. It was a quiet sector. The second battalion was in support positions near a town called Neufmaisons. It was news to the I, L, and M gangs to hear that we were in reserve. The faint theme song of artillery seemed to add truth to the story.

The troops got busy at once, practicing with the new Chauchat rifles. Guns chattered as gunners fired away at a muddy creek bank near town. Extended-order drills across boggy fields were the next form of torture.[6] Men were busy in spare time scraping the mud off firearms and equipment.

A batch of mail was wafted into this forlorn hole of mud and snow. A letter from June was forwarded by the other Hugh in Issoudun. He had written on the inside flap of the envelope, "Who's the lucky lady?" Men and fellow officers got a big kick out of a draft questionnaire, which I received from home. An evening was spent around madame's stove, thinking up crazy answers to the draft board's interrogations. How far away it all seemed. My mail was followed by an invitation to a loft billet to share a cake with some of the men. Corpl. Russell, of Barney's platoon, was delegated to bring me over. "Would I come?" from the gentlemanly corporal. I responded in a normal manner, exulting inwardly, "Would I salute Gen. Pershing?" It was in the candlelit barn loft that I learned about the men around me. Some were from Iowa farms, some from the railroad machine shops of Council Bluffs. Others were from Keokuk and the stockyards of Sioux City. Mahoney, Johns, Weiner, Parker,

Wickland, the Greek, and others made me welcome. Ghostly shadows danced on the stable wall, as the group bragged about Parker's gifts as a hypnotist. He had entertained the men at Camp Mills and during the long ago sea voyage. He agreed to put on a show for the new officers at the first opportunity. Men of other platoons climbed into the haymow and a good time was had by all. I returned to billets on air.

Sessions at mess found Capt. Clifton and the blatant Langworthy in disagreement about many things. The captain did not believe we would ever get to the front. Langworthy told him not to kid himself by a reference to the value of insurance and a crap-shooting snap of the thumb, "Plenty o' these—e'll throw a natural for ten thousand bucks, 'fore th' show is over." Another rift threatened when men were challenged by a dirty, full- breasted woman. We had better speak to our platoons about these things, the captain thought. "Scare them to death—give them hell," our superior ordered. Langworthy felt differently—"better show 'em th' g.u., stations first an' give 'em hell afterwards."[7]

A corridor in the Hôtel de Ville was crowded with muddy officers. Maj. Bronson strutted up and down importantly. The slow-moving Cullen was the last to tramp in, in response to the major's orders. The beetle-browed officer smothered a desire to "skin" Cullen and proceeded to business: "Well, men, it's happened." A hush pervaded the corridor. "What's happened?" officers inquired of each other, by eye. The major continued: "The Boche raided our first battalion at dawn—nineteen of our men were killed!" Officers communicated with each other again by lifting eyebrows. "So that's what all the fuss was about this morning." Maj. Bronson finished the few details at his disposal. Capt. McHugh was among the slaughtered. A Stokes mortar crew, supporting our troops, had been blown to smithereens by a direct hit on their ammunition dump.[8] The Boche had penetrated our trenches in one place and Smith had acquitted himself nobly.

We filed into the slushy street, awestruck. Groups of men gossiped about the tragedy. They seemed to know more about it than their battalion commander. Some seemed agape at the terrible news. Others shook their fists toward the front and cursed unknown Germans. A fellow shouted "We're rarin' to go."

A battalion runner sought me in billets that gloomy, heavy-laden evening. An order stated that Turk, Setliffe, and I were to proceed to Neufmaisons, on billeting detail, next morning. The second battalion was to relieve the first in the trenches, while we were to take their place in Neufmaisons—that was the way the gang around the stove interpreted the news. M company was to remain in "Mudville" for some mysterious reason.

I left the crowd in madame's kitchen talking it over and found the little church at the corner. A feeble sanctuary lamp flickered before the dark altar. A pew creaked. Outside passers-by with a lantern created a faint suggestion of a stained-glass window. Into the murky night again, I stumbled into Langworthy. He grunted with expletives about the quality of the darkness. Artillery rumbled faintly to the north. A squad floundered past us singing:

Apres la guerre fini,
'Merican soljer parti–
Madamaselle in uh fam-i-ly way,
Apres la guerre fini.

Turk, Setliffe, Keyser, a machine-gun officer, and I were off early, Turk in command. We climbed over the hill into Baccarat. A few early shoppers mingled with groups of French, American, and Italian soldiers. A civilian used a latrine, head and feet showing above and below the iron grating. We turned a corner. A gaunt block of smoky walls confronted us, untouched buildings standing prominently among the ruins. The tip of a church steeple, a shell hole high up, seemed undecided whether to stand or fall. A camion labored manfully by, towing a huge howitzer with caterpillar wheels. A company of muddy poilus trooped past. Six trumpeters in front, with long, straight instruments draped with red banners, might have dropped from the Middle Ages. Trumpets were placed to lips.

A clarion call split the raw morning air. I placed the music years later at a performance of the opera "Aida." We tramped across the bridge, turned left, and made our way to the Neufmaisons road.

A blanket of dirty, lace-like snow fringed our home-to-be. Farm wagons stood in front of sundry barns. A group of doughboys made their toilet in a horse trough, native women wringing garments in neighboring compartments. Shells swished to a hill above town and exploded with a bang. Answering guns thump-thumped in the same vicinity. Two camions appeared, as we waited for an M.P. officer in front of a manger guard room. Their burdens of pine boxes, covered with American flags and tricolors, were awesomely suggestive. A soldier confirmed our suspicions that the killed of yesterday were on their way to Baccarat and burial.

Billeting was accomplished in streets filled with French, Italians, and Americans. We caught a glimpse of Smith and a platoon caked from head to foot with dry mud. He answered our staccato questions a bit dazed and weary, "Boy, it's hell up there. I'm tellin' you!" An irascible woman chided B company men as they climbed from her lofts.

A great deal can happen in ninety-six hours.

The third battalion was now settled in Neufmaisons. Two artillerymen had been killed on the hill above town. Lieut. Williams of the sanitary department had described the gore to a wide-eyed group in front of billets. Capt. Clifton had remarked at mass that Capt. Doss of M had a drag with Maj. Bronson. M would get all the soft details as a result. This same M company had rolled into Neufmaisons with a hair-raising account of their raid into Boche trenches. Seven killed and twenty-two wounded was the price paid for three prisoners from a Uhlan regiment. Cullen described the battle to a wide-eyed crew. Two Germans had refused to leave their dugout and had been treated to a shower of bombs. Mack displayed a notebook he had carried in a pocket over his left nipple. A stray bullet had imbedded itself in the leaves. Both Cullen and Mack assured us that Van had been only slightly wounded.

A batch of K, L, and I officers had been to the front on observation. Capt. Clifton had gone to the Baccarat hospital sick. Langworthy had taken command of the company. Turk, Tim, Setliffe, and High were to go up next. Malcolm and I were to go up with them.

We met after breakfast mess with light packs and questioning hearts. Artillery on the hill was busy as we departed. Men of L surrounded the mess shack. My feelings were a strange mixture of contradictions. Fear I felt, yes, but it was modified greatly by a deep-seated curiosity. I had been deeply impressed with the sights and happenings of the past few days—the tragedy of the first battalion; those camions filled with dead; the fact that one so close as Van could actually be wounded. But after all, those were the things that happened to other people. Besides, what more could a fellow want? Gangs of men at the mess shack had bade us good-bye in affectionate fashion. Malcolm had just received a thrilling send-off as the six of us tramped toward the horse trough. And now L company men were singing again:

> *Eins, zwei, drei, vier,*
> *Thompson's gonna buy th' beer—*
> *Here is to Thompson,*
> *He's a dam' fine man.*

CHAPTER FIVE

The Trenches

Turk, High, Tim, Setliffe, Malcolm, and I made the hill above Neufmaisons on the way to the front. We fixed our gas masks at alert. Patches of stubborn snow fringed the Pexonne-Badonviller road and spotted the rolling fields ahead.

I meditated with pride over the send-off the men had given us and only sensed that the day was "fair and warmer." I indulged in a bit of mental singing—

> *Here is to Thompson,*
> *For Thompson, he's a man.*
> *Here is to Thompson,*
> *On th' corner he—*

The whiz of a shell left the tune unfinished. We fell over each other in a roadside ditch as a "77" exploded with a bang behind us.[1] Unseen batteries in a clump of woods thump-thumped when we picked ourselves up, joshing each other nervously.

We passed into a strip of road, shielded on the left by a wall of camouflage. A pioneer detail patched a broken place with tree boughs.[2] A deserted barn appeared and vanished behind us. The wall of camouflage became two walls farther on. In the open again and shells swished into the fields, exploding with muffled booms. Rounding a series of curves, we sighted a cluster of buildings just ahead.

Doughboys and poilus moved about lazily in Pexonne. A few village grownups and children carried French gas masks. An American sentinel stood at the gate of a modest Hôtel de Ville. Shells whizzed and swished over intermittently as we hit the road for Badonviller. More muddy road, more shells and an outline of shattered buildings brought the first leg of our journey to an end.

A narrow street, lined with wreckage, crossed the road terminus at right angles. A handful of French and doughboys hung about a rolling kitchen, housed in a badly smashed stable. Heavy timbers bolstered the shell-scarred walls of adjoining wreckage.

A group of dirty soldiers left the kitchen and came toward us. They were the guides, who were to take us to the front-line positions. The others went off with their escorts, while Malcolm and I followed Wallace, a fellow lieutenant, whom we had not seen since the days of far-off Rimaucourt. Our muddy, unkempt guide made the most of his role of hardened veteran, who knew all about the strange sights around us. The pinkish building to the left was battalion headquarters, F and G companies occupied the battered town, E and H were in the trenches. Capt. Starr, of G, had been wounded the day before.

We followed Wallace up the street of ruins. A water cart rested by the gaunt front of a demolished house. Splintered roof, plaster, and broken furniture were heaped in a mound of debris. Crumbling walls surrounded other twisted masses of destruction. Entrances to dark cellars along the street were covered with hoods of corrugated iron, heavy stones, or sandbags. A shell banged ahead of us; its splinters, thrown heavenward, buzzed down like a swarm of angry bees. Our tin hats were greatly appreciated.

We entered a narrow passage between houses and took a path to a hillside road. A chow detail passed us carrying dirty slum containers on poles, from shoulder to shoulder. The detail obliqued around a snow-fringed and water-filled shell hole as we tramped by, toward a cottage whose roof had been torn by shellfire. Wallace led the way by a rustic grave and into a muddy gash in the hill. We squeezed by a cave-in of broken revetment and flattened ourselves against the trench wall to make room for passing doughboys and French soldiers. Slipping and sliding along the duckboards of a winding trench, we bumped our heads on the overhead cross pieces.[3] A seemingly endless quarter-mile of slick, uncertain footing brought us out into a small clearing, surrounded by anemic scrub oaks.

A netting of chicken wire, draped with artificial foliage, augmented the sparse natural cover. Lounging men puffed cigarettes around a group of dugout entrances. We stumbled down a steep dark stairway to one of the underground shelters.

A muddy officer pored over papers on a candlelit table. A chorus of snores came from a dark tier of bunks. The underground shelter was heavy with sewer-like odors. The officer, Capt. Bates, interpreted a map of the sector with a dirty finger. Here was Badonviller. This zigzagging line was the trench we had just come through. And the black dot here was the dugout we were in. This map mark and another like it, to the left, were about midway in the system of zigzagging lines, spread fan-shape in front of the spot marked Badonviller. Other winding lines ran from the company dugouts to the trenches ahead. Each loop of trenches in front was connected by communicating lines. Each loop represented a platoon strong point, dots indicating the platoon dugouts. The strong points were designated on the map by French names and a combination of initials and numbers. It was easier to remember that the dugout we were in was called PA5 than to remember its French designation. Platoon positions were more readily identified by their lettered and initialed markings, from left to right, GC9, GC10, GC11, and GC12.

The captain finished his instructions. A series of lines in red pencil marked the German trenches. They seemed to be fairly close opposite GC9 and GC10, swerving away where GC11 projected out into a small salient and still farther away opposite the loop of trenches marked GC12.[4] Machine-gun positions to the back of us were identified. The French held the adjoining sector to the right and H company manned GC11 and GC12.

A shell thumped somewhere above us, shaking the timber of the dugout, as we prepared to leave.

After climbing the dugout stairs, Wallace proceeded to show us around. We tried to take in everything explained for our benefit. The rusty klaxon horn at the dugout entrance was for gas alarms. A wooden rack held rocket signals. Wallace explained them: green for gas, six-star red for a twenty-minute barrage from supporting artillery, six-star white asked the artillery to lengthen its barrage, and three-star white signaled for the return of patrols and raiding parties in no man's land.[5] A test barrage from the artillery was secured by telephone signal from company or platoon dugouts. The words, "trial barrage," sent the distant battery or batteries into action with one shell in front of the signaling zone of front-line trenches.

Wallace continued to hand out useful information. Emergency rations of hardtack and bully beef were not to be opened without orders.[6] Sealed tins of emergency water in company and platoon dugouts were treated with like respect, chow details issuing a canteen ration daily. This supply had to serve for drinking, teeth-brushing, etc.

Messages between battalion headquarters and company and platoon positions were usually written and carried by runners. Liaison patrols constantly kept the isolated positions in touch with one another. The patrols also ensured that the connecting stretches of trench would be kept clear of all but friends.

We repeated the day's password, "Versailles." This would identify us to all sentinels. The answer or countersign, "Brittany," would seal the bargain. These signals were changed daily and Wallace explained how important they became after nightfall.

We left the clearing, skidded down a steep communicating trench, and crossed a low place. A bullet pinged overhead; Wallace grinned widely when Malcolm and I ducked in unison. Three shells swished over us in rapid succession and exploded in the direction of Badonviller. I began to get a bit uncomfortable over what was in store for us.

Floundering through mud, we crossed a brook, passed another rustic grave, and pulled up in front of a chicken-wire gate. A sentinel admitted us into another trench.

We splashed by a muddy group that worked with shovels in the trench bottom. Floundering around a corner, we came to a dugout and adjoining shelter, covered with sunken hoods of corrugated iron. A doughboy stood by the blanketed entrance to the dugout. Another, with rifle and bayonet, lay on his belly upon a pile of mud atop. We were at the platoon headquarters of GC9.

Wallace led us around a bayou and into a fire trench. The sight that greeted us brought an immediate and positive reaction. "Desolate" was the only name for it. A mass of rusty barbed wire was strung on crisscrosses of posts that seemed to grow from the ground. Ghost-like trees to the right were splattered with shell scars. Some had fallen into the mass of twisted wire and upturned earth. Others were broken off at various heights, like so many matchsticks. The expanse of desolation sloped up a gentle rise. The German trenches were hidden behind the crest some two hundred yards or more away.

We retraced our difficult steps, following our guide to the neighboring platoon positions. We lurched down soupy, demolished trenches toward GC10. Men in rubber boots, hip high, grunted with shovels, here and there. Others worked in the tangles of mud, splintered stanchions, broken telephone cable, and twisted iron. A Boche plane buzzed overhead as we approached a dark cavity in the earth filled with splintered debris. It was the place where Capt. McHugh had been killed in the German bombardment of the first battalion.

Doughboys with automatic rifles were in outposts jutting out along the line. Two men sat at each gun, while another pair slept under metal and sandbag shelters, close at hand. A heavily manned outpost between GC10 and GC11 had its gun set up among the ruins of a farmhouse with the muzzle stuck through a wide slit in a tumbled-down chimney. More men slept in a water-logged cellar below. A German helmet hung from a spike in the chimney's mortar, raw flesh and tufts of black hair protruding from the lining.

Wallace took us into GC11, which was out of his company sector. He had a special reason. We were greeted by a sickening odor, as he led us around a turn in a sloppy ditch. The body of a dead German, in muddy, green-gray overcoat lay on the trench bottom. I felt a spasm of nausea at the unexpected sight of what had been a man. The face was mud-smeared and distorted, the head a sickening livid, where the decomposed scalp had come off. The Boche had been killed during the recent raid on the first battalion. The body had been recovered from in front of GC11 and buried in a sump hole, wrapped in a blanket, but had been dug up by a detail from regimental intelligence and identified as a member of the Fifteenth Bavarian Storm Battalion.

I staggered back to GC10 behind Wallace and Malcolm, thinking of the gruesome figure. What kind of fellow had that thing been? Was he married? Maybe there were some kids somewhere, away off there to the north, who waited for him to come home.

A liaison patrol passed us with the news that an American had been shot in GC12. We listened awestruck to the hurried details. The fellow had stood at the dugout entrance after delivering a message. A sniper's bullet or a stray one had pierced the area of the heart, killing him instantly.

I had little stomach for the greasy slum that arrived soon after Wallace had left us with Lieut. McCarthy to the sewer-like shelter of GC10. Men filed out in the late afternoon with mess tins. A group of muddy Frenchmen were with them. Cigarettes were doused as a pair struggled up with the heavy slum containers. A third man followed with a tow sack of bread, cut into huge hunks. Another filled canteens from a water bag, after the men had finished chow and wiped slimy tins clean with wads of paper or bread crusts.

Shells landed between us and PA5, while the chow detail made its departure. Occasional bursts of machine-gun fire reverberated up and down the dusk-laden expanse of desolation. It was dark when we entered McCarthy's shelter again. A candle flickered on a small table. Water was ankle deep under the tiers of shadowy bunks. A sergeant appeared and asked Malcolm and me if we cared to join him in an inspection of outposts. If the atmosphere of the trenches had been impressive by day, a deep, all-pervading eeriness accompanied the clammy mantle of darkness.

We splashed after Sgt. Brown to a series of posts. Silent doughboys stood on the fire steps, peering out into the dark night. A few poilus stood with them, seemingly without moving a muscle. Klaxon horns barked in the distance. An occasional flare outlined ghostly cross-sections of wire. Rifle fire cracked from distant parts of the inky blackness.

Floundering around in the mud from post to post, we were halted by nervous hisses from sentinels. The blood-curdling commands were followed by a spluttered password and a whispered countersign. Sgt. Brown left us in an outpost, where Malcolm and I decided to remain for experience.

The night wore on, as we shook with cold and nervousness by the side of our invisible companions. Shadowy posts took on lifelike forms and seemed to move. Wire clinked faintly in the wind, to send shivers up and down the spine. More clinking and I was startled by a shot from one of the group. We all joined in, firing into the black nothingness. A doughboy whispered: "Boche!" A shadowy Frenchman shrugged: "Pas Boche!"[7] The Americans were unconvinced. There was another volley of Springfield and pistol fire. A fellow beside me crumpled into the mud with a groaning oath. A commotion took place in the trench bottom. Malcolm and I considerately volunteered to help the wounded man to McCarthy's dugout. In the candlelight we discovered with relief that only a slight scalp wound had resulted from a bullet, which had pierced the man's helmet from front to back. Excitement subsided as stretcher-bearers helped the injured man to PA5 and Malcolm and I returned to the outpost. A whispered argument about the shooting ceased as dark figures inquired with suppressed excitement about their wounded buddy.

The gray light of dawn added a new note to no man's land. The full force of GC10 "stood to," according to orders that called for an alert from an hour before dawn until full daylight.[8] The gray view ahead revealed nothing more than the dismal scene of yesterday. The new day crept forth by almost imperceptible jumps, as though some human hand was manipulating the lighting effects upon a barren stage. A rumble from the distant west grew into a hovering thunder, then softened. It grew voluminous again. It seemed for a moment that the far-away bombardment was right at us. A neighboring outpost began to fire nervously. We were startled by a six-star red flare that spewed heavenward from the direction of McCarthy's dug-out. An avalanche of artillery descended in front of us. "Boche! Boche!" a man shouted, as mud and wire went skyward. A Frenchman made a hurried reconnaissance while the banging continued. He returned and shrugged: "Pas Boche!" The out-post reveled in the spectacle of bursting shells and flying mud. For twenty minutes the exciting show continued. It paused momentarily and came to a close with a brace of 75's that screamed down into the wire in front of us.[9]

Sgt. Brown floundered up with breathless explanations. A messenger from a neighboring outpost had panted into McCarthy's dugout with the startling news that gray figures were crawling over the wire-banded crest in front of his po-sition. The unnerved McCarthy had called the artillery into action without investigating.

Malcolm and I caught a little sleep after breakfast and then relieved Lieut. Little, who had been sent from PA5 to relieve the panicky McCarthy.

The day proved uneventful until Wallace appeared in the late afternoon with prospective excitement. Our old friend Sawyer, in Badonviller with G company, had been ordered to repair the wire in front of GC9, after nightfall. Wallace himself was to protect Sawyer's crowd with a covering party. Did we want to go along? Well, there was only one answer a fellow could give, under the circumstances.

Wallace herded his gang of fifteen together. We tramped along to find Sawyer the center of an idolizing group of muddy men near the platoon dugout of GC9. The doughboys dumped stakes, mallets, and rolls of wire at a command from their burly leader. Sawyer proceeded to toss grenades to the wait-ing men, like so many baseballs. The ominous "pineapples" were caught with a forced air of nonchalance. I was much relieved when the big fellow handed us our quota of two apiece. The two gangs struggled through the dusk to GC9's easternmost outpost to wait for dark.

We climbed over the dark sandbags and into no man's land. A few yards out in the blackness and the distance seemed ten times greater than reality. We continued to crawl forward, each man groping for the man ahead. We became tangled in wire as Sawyer's crowd followed noisily, dragging their unwieldy burdens. A flare lighted the area around us. We lay transfixed. A man behind me panted heavily and I was relieved to learn that I was not alone with my shaky feelings. Wallace crawled from nowhere and whispered instructions to form in a semicircle. Another flare! An interminable period of quiet. Sawyer and his gang got busy with their stakes and mallets. There was a rattling of wire and smothered curses. The hammering of mallets on stakes split the inky darkness. Somebody whispered nervously, "My God, them ———s 'll wake up th' kaiser." The hammering ceased suddenly; a distant echo of hammering came from the German section of the darkness. "Thump, thump, thump!" came the weird sounds from the night. Sawyer's crowd commenced again and ceased after ages; again came the spooky echoes.

A welcome hiss, after an eternity in the freezing mud, and we headed homeward. More wire! Cut, bruised, and covered with mud, we fell into the waiting oupost, heaving sighs of relief. Malcolm and I thanked our hosts with fake enthusiasm. They grunted, "So long," and disappeared in the darkness.

Another night on post, another gray dawn, and a hurried mess tin of slum finished our tour of inspection. We labored up the trenches to PA5 and on through the shell-torn town of Badonviller. We met the other observers who had come out just ahead of us. Hitting the muddy road toward Neufmaisons, we tramped wearily across a drab countryside. I drank deeply of the foggy morning air. Life seemed mighty sweet as the mud-caked group plodded on beyond Pexonne to prepare for the third battalion's first hitch in the trenches.

Lieutenant Thompson's identity card. Courtesy Hugh S. Thompson, M.D.

Lt. Hugh S. Thompson, at right. Courtesy Hugh S. Thompson, M.D.

Sergeant Price and Master Engineer Hudson holding the Rainbow Division flag as it is unfurled at Rolampont, February 3, 1918. Courtesy U.S. Army Signal Corps.

1st Battalion, 168th Infantry Regiment, Rolampont. Courtesy U.S. Army Signal Corps.

Franco-American patrol under Lt. John M. Currie going out into "no man's land," Badonviller, March 17, 1918. Courtesy U.S. Army Signal Corps.

Gen. Charles T. Menoher and Secretary of War Newton D. Baker,
March 19, 1918. Courtesy U.S. Army Signal Corps.

General Menoher and Col. Douglas MacArthur. Courtesy U.S. Army
Signal Corps.

Lieutenant Currie surveying the terrain prior to a trench raid, April or May 1918. Courtesy U.S. Army Signal Corps.

CHAPTER SIX

More of Same

Back in Neufmaisons after a glimpse of a "quiet sec tor," rest and hearty companionship erased the images of mud, wire, and desolation. It was not for long. Platoon commanders were immediately busy getting rid of cooties and trying to pass on to the men the knowledge gained of life in the trenches.

Each member of my army of fifty-odd was now a familiar individual, from Sgt. McDonough to the lowly Chink. My uncertain spirits were bucked up by an affectionate respect that lured me into thinking that I could stand anything. The test came suddenly. Two days later the murky blackness of 3:00 A.M. found the battalion on the Pexonne-Badonviller road, marching at intervals of one hundred yards between platoons.

A puzzling confusion took place in the pitch-black town just behind the trenches. Shells banged intermittently as the battalion buckled, shuffled, and halted. Kitchens were set up in a demolished building and a chow detail from Cherub's platoon and my own left in charge of Sgt. Kling. Groping single file, each man holding the coat-tail of the man ahead, the silent troops slipped along the zigzagging trench toward PA5. Swishing enemy shells, answering batteries, and a helpless fear accompanied the night relief.

Daylight found M and I companies occupying Badonviller and K holding the ditches and dugouts of PA6, GC11, and GC12. We had taken over the positions which Malcolm and I had lately left so eagerly. Barney was in the mudhole called GC9 with the first platoon. Malcolm held GC10 with the second. Cherub and I found ourselves at the company headquarters, PA5, with Langworthy, Sgt. Runyan, and some seventy men. Wallace, of E company, told me in passing that a patrol had stumbled on the body of a Frenchman in front of GC10 during the night. The gray figures that had so recently startled McCarthy's platoon had been allies instead of enemies. The panic at dawn had cost a friendly life. E company pulled out and our first hitch was under way.

Doughboys seemed to fall naturally into the strange routine. Front-line groups immediately formed a maze of barricades around the mudhole positions. Tin cans or an old cow bell, hung on barbed wire at strategic points, meant a dead giveaway for unsuspecting prowlers. Chow details labored manfully up the winding ditches. Slum was often spilled en route, due to Boche shelling. Picturesque language followed from the hungry men out front. Cherub and I supervised these food details and the pick-and-shovel groups who struggled to keep the muddy gashes passable. Runners and liaison patrols kept in touch with battalion headquarters and the isolated forward positions. We were busy by night penciling messages in the candlelit depths of our dugout, at Langworthy's dictation. Night working parties, patrols, a Stokes mortar crew in a nearby clump of woods, and the French on our right were involved in our situation. Ammunition must be checked and reported to Maj. Bronson. All "memos" between units were read and initialed by subordinates, much after the fashion of a large business organization.

In the midst of these activities Langworthy gave me a job that filled me with trepidation. The wire in front of GC9's eastern outpost had been cut for the passage of M company's raid. An abandoned trench had been divested of hoops of protective wire for the same purpose. I was to lead an ambush patrol each night to guard the head of the old trench from dusk until daylight.

Cherub, Wolf, Ackerson, and Mahoney went to the outpost with me for a daylight reconnaissance. A gun crew watched us climb over their sandbags and into the old trench. We crept forward until the ditch became impassable. A cautious peep revealed an expanse of upturned earth, broken trees, and twisted wire. In plain view, some fifty yards away, was the parapet of a German trench familiar to us from maps.[1] The trench was thought to be occupied by the Boche at night.

The juvenile Cherub immediately placed me in an embarrassing position. Why not crawl over for the exploration? I tried to put a damper on this crazy plan without betraying my real feelings. The others seemed enthusiastic about the venture. Before I knew it we were jumping from shell hole to shell hole, armed with pistols and a grenade apiece. I could hardly swallow for suppressed excitement. Beads of cold perspiration dampened the lining of my helmet. A final agony of difficult crawling and I lay on my belly looking into a deep, well-revetted trench. A ladder lay on the trench bottom. A wooden fire step was directly below us. A shelter entrance to the right attracted Cherub's attention. We dropped into the trench cat-like. We tiptoed toward the shelter. Cherub stuck his "45" inside and followed its muzzle. The rest of us entered after him. Picks, shovels, and boxes of German "pigeon egg" grenades were scattered about in the musty half-light. We hurriedly filled our pockets with grenades, grabbed a tool apiece, and made ready to vanish. Wolf discovered a light Maxim gun on a fire step around a bayou.[2] Four of us climbed out and relieved Wolf of his burden. We pulled him to safety and scurried across no man's land, hearts in mouth. The outpost was pop-eyed when we landed behind their sandbags. At PA5 men ganged around to examine the booty and to ask excited questions. Langworthy appeared and gave us the devil. His foghorn castigations only stimulated the men's admiration of our foray. Frightened out of my wits shortly before, I now puffed with a delighted vanity. I hardly heard Langworthy's profane assurances that it would be "the States for us, toot sweet," if we ever pulled such a damned fool stunt again.

After routine work by day, the ambush patrol in front of the old trench had spent interminable nights in the freezing blackness. Wolf's automatic rifle team, Owen, Ackerson, Britt,

Mahoney, and others, made up the detail. A snatch of sleep in the dirty dugout bunks by morning, work details by afternoon, and we repeated the patrol each night from dusk until daylight. Crawling from man to man in the freezing indigo, fear kept me awake for hours. Nature would then assert itself. Numb with cold, senses deadened by the monotonous stillness, and I would find myself in a trance, with eyes open. A flare, the crack of rifle fire, a suspicious noise would jerk me into needles and pins again. A series of trances and periods of fearful wakefulness strung out the long hours. Back to the dugout, I slept the sleep of the dead for an hour or perhaps two, only to have Langworthy shake me into a state of semi-stupor.

A series of events and the overpowering weariness turned into a terrific tension of tired body and wide-awake nerves. Malcolm and his platoon had had a patrol scare in front of one of their outposts. News of the German trench had put battalion headquarters on the qui vive.[5] A memorandum came from Badonviller one morning stating that a large raiding party from I, K, and M companies was to raid for prisoners in the afternoon. A bombardment was to precede the dash into the German trench. I was to conduct the usual ambush patrol after the raiding party had finished its mission.

I led my gang of ten into GC9 ahead of time. They waited in a deep, water-logged sap with most of Barney's men.[4] Three outposts manned the strong point to scan the wire ahead. Russell guarded the entrance to the deep sap. Carling lay on the pile of mud above Barney's shelter.

Threads of a dreamlike past sprung from the quagmire called GC9. Barney had two visitors up for observation from the Ninth Infantry. Capt. Gill proved to be a West Point classmate of an acquaintance of mine. Pedigrees were swapped. A reference to Chattanooga brought Lieut. MacNider into action. Did I know Clifford Grayson? Did I know him! "Well," said MacNider, "he's in my battalion and an A1 officer." "Well, what do you know about that!" I mused. A Signal Corps man from Barney's dugout, overhearing our conversation, asked if I knew his nephew, Xavier Kuss, from home, who died on the border. Xavier and I had sat in adjoining desks at Baylor for several years.[5] "Well, I'll be damned," I mused again as Stokes mortars and others of French variety began pounding the German trenches.

We watched the tense raiding party file by to their jumping-off place. Stokes mortar shells toppled lazily overhead and banked into the unseen German positions. French "pigs," huge bombs with percussion caps and guiding fins, looped over gracefully and ended in thunder. Whining fragments flew back toward us. I thought of the unlucky raiders and thanked my lucky stars that I was not with them.

MacNider requested permission to climb on the dugout top where he could see the show better. He came down and Barney relieved Carling. The latter took Russell's place at the sap entrance and we boosted Russell to the dugout top. He lay on his belly upon the pile of mud.

He was hardly settled before a German shell whizzed over, banked into the brook behind us, and drenched us with a shower of muddy water. Whiz-bangs followed in rapid succession.[6] We sought the trench bottom in a panic. There was a deadening explosion in a nearby bayou. Shells screamed and whistled, filling me with a fear that I had never known before. More shells whistled into the brook. An angry express train flashed above us.[7] Suddenly all became quiet!

I picked myself up, my mouth dry and stomach fluttering. Barney's voice brought me to myself. "Where is Russell?" he asked anxiously. I had forgotten all about Russell and the others. Grenades began bursting in the direction the raiders had taken. A wraithlike cloud of acrid smoke floated above us. We climbed on top of the shelter to find a gaping shell hole. Barney fell into a frenzy of concern over the missing Russell. He berated himself for not taking care of his sentinel. We tried to console him. If it hadn't been Russell it would have been Carling—and MacNider, too, if the latter hadn't climbed down just in time. Capt. Gill and MacNider took charge while Barney and I looked hurriedly through the bayous for the missing man. We jerked up startled! There, just in front of us, a human arm rested on a strip of parados; an arm in a brown overcoat sleeve.[8] The limb breathed with personality. It might have been Russell himself. The hand, with gray glove turned back, in "dandy" fashion, drooped gracefully. A livid joint protruded from the other end of brown rags. There was little blood. Some monstrous giant had wrenched the arm right out of its socket. I was sick with an indescribable sorrow. The war for the first time seemed useless. Was this part of the boy whom I had just helped to boost to the mud pile? Days passed like seconds in a mental kaleidoscope. Could this be the arm stretched out to me in the "Mudville" hayloft? Was that the friendly hand that had held a hunk of cake, waiting for me to receive it?

Barney picked up the limb carefully and hid it behind the parados, with the hurried request that I search farther after I had come off patrol in the morning.

Gunnery had ceased when we went back to the dugout. A nod answered the inquiring eyes of the visitors and Carling. Members of the raiding party stumbled by, breathless, panting that they had failed to bag any prisoners. "Th'————s must a-knowed we wuz comin'!" A tail-end group staggered up, helping three bloody doughboys. Capt. Moore, of I company, brought up the rear. He jerked his head toward the outpost and shouted nervously, in passing: "You got a dead man out there!"

My gang came out of the deep sap wide-eyed, but quiet. I told them about Russell, trying to whip myself and them into a frenzy that would carry us through the awful night ahead. Some were silent. Others gripped their Springfields and muttered curses against the Germans. We made our difficult way to the outpost and crawled into the abandoned trench. We had covered some thirty yards when we discovered a man sitting on the trench bottom. He leaned against the bank, his back toward us. The stub of an arm stuck in the trench wall. The absence of an overcoat identified him as a member of the raiding party. They had run right by one of their number in their excitement. The man's left leg was bare from hip to wrap legging. A big, dark fellow, he seemed to be sleeping serenely. Wolf posted the patrol, while the redheaded Owen and I prepared to move the dead man. Owen secured a shelter half from the outpost.[9] I grabbed the large figure in the collar and dragged him on the canvas. The bare leg toppled into the trench with a sickening thud. Falling dusk added to an overwhelming horror. I picked up the heavy leg. It flexed at the knee and nearly threw me off balance as I threw it beside the gruesome body with an "Ugh!" A helmet and twisted rifle followed. An exploding grenade sack at the hip had caused the terrible tragedy. Owen and I dragged the collection of remains through the dusk. Men on the outpost helped us get it over the parapet of sandbags. A squad left a nearby shelter and dropped to hands and knees for a better view as Owen and I struggled by them. A clipped aluminum disc in the shelter's candlelight revealed that the soldier was James T. Marshall, of M company. Two of Barney's men and Frenchmen from GC6 carried the body to PA5. I spent a horrible night with the ambush patrol in the ghostly darkness.

The patrol splashed up the communicating trench toward the company dugout. Mahoney and Gross carried all that was left of Russell. Two arms, two legs, and a mangled trunk in a torn overcoat rested separately under a muddy tent half. A tent rope kept the mangled pile in place. We had looked high and low for Russell's head without success. It must have fallen into one of the many water-filled shell holes.

We swapped places with the litter and finally made the clearing, where our burden was deposited to await removal. A shell whizzed over and banged in Badonviller. Men came out of the dugouts and milled about silently with a mixture of awkward concern and morbid curiosity. Anderson, a seventeen-year-old buddy of Russell's, blubbered audibly. The illiterate, forty-year-old McCarter had, since the early days, evidenced a deep affection for the clean-cut fellow whose pieces rested under the canvas. McCarter now knelt beside the muddy litter. He removed his helmet in reverence. Other helmets followed. Rifle fire cracked in the distance. A hush fell over the gathering. McCarter's voice, vibrant with feeling, broke the morning stillness. "You poor ————! You poor ————!"

M and I companies relieved us the day after Russell and Marshall were killed. Mark and Cullen took over Barney's and Malcolm's positions. We splashed back to Badonviller, drenched to the skin by a pouring rain. We fell into the town's dark cellars. Langworthy, Malcolm, and I shared a dingy basement with McDonough, Stowers, Bartram, Wolf, and Owen. The smell of musty earth pervaded the place. Walls of heavy stone were covered with a sickly whitewash. A small crucifix hung on a nail in the mortar, evidently left by Frenchmen. The company was strewn about the street in similar underground shelters.

The first night a can of corned beef and cabbage fell from a pack hung on the dark well, giving Bartram a bad cut over an eye. He was soon back with a patch over the injured optic.

We fell into a new routine, tense and exhausted—"stand to" in the streets at dawn; work details in the communicating trenches; snatches of sleep in the afternoons; patrols in no man's land at night. Cherub caught one of the patrol jobs almost immediately. He took a picked detail of thirty-two men into a German trench near the one we had investigated. Ten of my men went with him. The outfit, equipped with bombs, gunnery, and reserve rations, was to lie in wait for possible Germans for thirty-six hours. The crowd had been on the job for two nights and a day when I received disturbing news in the depth of our cellar. I was to lead a combat patrol that night with twenty men of my own choosing. Our route was to take us out through the old familiar outpost, by the left flank of Cherub's position, to the lane between our wire and the Germans' and down the lane to the ravine in front of GC11. The journey was to end in that mudhole.

Most of my old patrol formed the nucleus of the new one. We had not crawled far into the pitch blackness before I discovered that some of the twenty men were missing. A whispered consultation with McDonough and we decided to go on without them. Someone would say we were yellow if we didn't. We crawled forward on our bellies into the slimy blackness. We neared the general location of Cherub and his ambushers. We were about to skirt their flank, some fifty yards to our right, when a shot came from their direction. A bedlam of rifle fire and grenades developed. Automatic rifles chattered angrily. We hugged the mud as bullets pinged over us. A red flare from the German part of the darkness popped toward us and spewed out a few feet away. The booming flashes to our right seemed to last for an eternity. It ceased suddenly. We waited for ages. We crawled forward again and then turned left, scrambling through patches of upturned wire. We finally made what we thought to be our westerly destination. A few movements and we had completely lost our orientation. I was filled with an inward panic. Was that dark patch over there Germany or home? Whispered arguments followed in the darkness, men dropping official formalities. "It's this way, Tommy," assured the husky voice of McDonough. Wolf took whispered issue. "No, it ain't, Tommy, it's over here." I felt a trifle better for the familiarity.

There was nothing to do but try one of the directions. We crawled forward cautiously, untangling ourselves from strands of wire. We inched along farther. A gun flashed almost in our faces. We hugged the mud for dear life. A stage whisper came from the darkness in front of us, "Boches out there!" A loud voice in my ear startled me out of my wits, "Let us in, you dam' fools, we're Americans!" We tumbled into the farmhouse outpost between GC10 and GC11. Pierce was dispatched to GC11 to let the platoon there know that we were in safely. The lost men were waiting for us in Mack's dugout at GC10. They had been afraid to go on after losing us for fear that we would bump into each other. Had they said anything about getting lost? Only to Mack, was the answer. "Good—don't say anything about it," I cautioned.

Back in the candlelight of the pink chateau that was battalion headquarters Lieut. Kry, the intelligence officer, handed me a penciled sketch of the trenches. I was to trace the path we had taken. I proceeded to trace, instead, the path we were supposed to have taken, noting in my report the shooting from Cherub's gang. I added a plausible story in writing. I walked wearily and trembling to the cellar at 61 Grande Rue, making the mental notation: "What Kry doesn't know won't hurt him!"

Muffled sounds of hilarity came from the dark cellars along the street. My cellar companions greeted me heartily. They had rustled a supply of Prunella, a "white lightning" distilled from prunes. The stuff was fiery, but it erased unwanted pictures and relieved the terrific tension. Most of the crowd were soon groggy. A shell banged in the street and Wolf thumbed his nose at the cellar stairway. Another bang and Stowers yelled drunkenly: "Gimme his rations!" The serious Malcolm watched our antics with a half-amused aloofness. Malcolm had his own inner resources and his own code, but he was tolerant of the codes of others. Muffled laughter bounced off the candlelit wall as Stowers decorated Bartram with a piece of tin hung on a string. The medal was for valor in the "Battle of Bully Beef." The maudlin crowd crawled from their damp blankets to try some close harmony. The singing was a failure. McDonough tried a solo of "My Little Gray Home in the West." His plaintive tenor touched tender spots and he was interrupted brutally: "Outside with that stuff! Can it!"

Langworthy's rich baritone described his respect for the simple faith of the Frenchmen. He toasted the crucifix from the neck of a bottle. No wonder you couldn't lick these here Frogs.[10] They had a real religion. The foghorn voice, mellowed by rum, continued its admiration—"Everywhere you go in th' lousy country, they got Jesus on a stick!"

Cherub and his bedraggled gang turned up next morning. Britt, of my platoon, had been sent to the Baccarat hospital with a couple of mangled fingers. Mahoney, with a wound in the shoulder and a bad leg wound, had been brought out of the old German trench on a section of duckboard. The crowd told us all there was to tell about the scrap in the darkness. "No, they hadn't seen nothin'." Somebody started shooting without orders. They had just thrown all the grenades they could and the Boche had thrown a few on their own account.

Gas shells crashed into Badonviller after nightfall. The misty air was filled with barking klaxons. We suffocated in the cellar at 61 Grande Rue and finally dropped into a fitful sleep with our masks on.

Heaven descended upon us next day. The horizon blue of the French 169th Infantry swarmed in to relieve us. We departed worn out, but happy, the Frenchmen greeting us and saying good-bye at the same time: "Amèricain–bon! La guerre, pas bon!" grunted the overly welcome poilus.[11]

We hiked mechanically to Neufmaisons and on to Deneuvre, a village above Baccarat, for the night. Seven kilometers the following morning took us to a village called Bru and to the delightful world of rest and sleep and peace.

CHAPTER SEVEN

To Bru and Back

A spring sun lavished itself upon the village of Bru. Men of the second and third battalions wallowed in its friendly rays. Chickens and geese strutted about unconcerned with the affairs of the new arrivals. The smell of animals, even the luscious manure piles, was welcome after the stinking trenches.

A block of smoked walls testified to a bit of 1914 history. Evidently the torch had been used hurriedly. A creek lined with poplars wound through fields of pastoral beauty near our moss-covered barn and dwelling billet. Our slatternly hostess had her hands full with seven dirty children.

What a lazy, carefree life was that back there in the department of Vosges where artillery meant only an occasional and distant rumble. Langworthy expressed it perfectly. It was great to get the mud off your lungs.

Soldiers splashed about in the chilly creek, its banks lined with an audience of French children. Cooties were drowned and egg-nits cremated by applying a match flame to the seams of underwear. There was a variety of deep satisfactions. Short setting-up exercises after a late breakfast were followed by days of loafing. Cigarettes and chocolate from Jack Eller, the "Y" man's open-air shop on the creek bridge, were consumed with relish.[1] Jack, a former pentathlon champion from the Irish- American Athletic Club, told us tales of the Olympic games. There was a journey to the neighboring village of

Jeanmenil to see men of M company receive the Croix de Guerre for their raid into the German trenches; pilgrimages to the quaint town of Rambervillers, with its dainty shops and cafés, its colorful crowds of Hindus, Annamese, English, Italian, French, and American soldiers.[2]

Of discipline there was none, but there was something: officers addressed each other by their first names or nicknames. Malcolm was Walter at first and then Wally. Talbot was John, Albert was Luke, Knabe the Rhodes scholar was a George, and so on. I was Tommy to all save Tim, who always called me Hughie. Some of the company commanders even called Maj. Bronson "Joe" and got away with it. And the cocky, hard-boiled Langworthy, how the devil had he ever gotten such a name as Percy? That's what the rest of us wanted to know. The answer was characteristic. It had been hung on the mortified bearer with his first pair of "three-cornered britches," pinned on with the first safety pin. How the hell could he help it? A laughing crowd decided that "Perce" would at least be some improvement over Percy. Perce proceeded to caution a tittering company about too much familiarity. Bru was lousy with eaves-dropping higher-ups, and it would be best to play safe. "Better keep th' Perce stuff for billets an' give us a snappy 'lootenant' in public."

A flock of mail came in. A paper called the *Stars and Stripes* flooded the village.[3] Chattanooga papers recorded a continued epidemic of marriages. Old friends were being caught in the "breeze," enlisting at Oglethorpe or preparing to go into the 30th Division.[4] My younger brother was headed for France with a tank company from home. Tim and I swapped notes and answered a batch of letters. Rambervillers was raided for presents for the homefolk. A beaded bag was dispatched to the faraway June.

An avalanche of rumors descended upon our peaceful surroundings. And what delightful ones! We were going to the Italian front. No, a long siege of rest was in store, while a complete American army was forming. Better than all this, the division was to be shipped home and paraded in every large city. A battalion meeting, which broke up a planned show by Parker the hypnotist, also shattered these beautiful illusions. Maj. Bronson was "short and sweet." The Boche had been raising Cain with the British in Picardy, wherever that was. The French needed every available veteran. We were not only going back to the ditches, we were going to take over the Baccarat sector completely. We would have to man just twice as much front as formerly.[5]

Doughboys swarmed the village of Deneuvre again. Sundry roofs and the torn church spire of Baccarat lay below us in the valley. Men and officers ganged the pillaged town for shopping. Friends were looked up in the gray hospital run by Sisters of Mercy. Capt. Clifton "goldbricked" in a soft bed. Terrell, the artillery lieutenant, who had lost a leg on the Neufmaisons hill, sat up for nourishment. Members of my platoon and I found Britt with bandages around his finger stubs. Mahoney was located in a private room.

The odor of antiseptic and dressings was oppressive as the small crowd of visitors closed the door behind them. A gray-faced figure sat up in bed, a Croix de Guerre pinned on his dirty jacket. A shoulder was heavily bandaged. Mahoney told us all about the medal. "Why, a dam' Frog general had th' guts to come in here with a gang and kiss me right before all of 'em."

Levity over, Mahoney wanted to talk to me alone. Would the other fellows wait outside? I closed the door at his request. A sheet was thrown back and I gazed upon a bandaged leg stump. Noting my shock, Mahoney was apologetic. He hadn't wanted to say anything to the others about it. Would I write a letter for him?

I scribbled the letter on "Y" paper, according to his dictation:

> France,
> Dear Mother—Am sending you a few lines to let you know I am getting along well. Am having the lieutenant arrange to have my insurance papers sent to you and to inquire about my allotment.
> We went to the trenches lately and I had a little accident. Was not very bad. Am in hospital and getting along fine. Will

have the lieutenant write again soon for me. Best love to you
and dad and all the kids from
Your son, HAROLD

I tried to persuade Ed, as "Harold" was known to his bud-
dies, to be more specific. It wouldn't hurt the folks to be prepared for what was under the bedclothes. Ed thought differently. I could say something in the letter if I wanted to, but the
leg part of it was forbidden. He didn't want 'em to worry—"Just
tell th' old man to oil up th' Ford an' lay in "beaucoo" gas. I'm
gonna split Sioux City wide open!"
    I added a line to Mrs. Mahoney. Harold seemed to be get-
ting along well. She was to call on me if there was anything
in the world I could do for either of them. A French Sister
came in with a tray and I left with a promise to come back on
the morrow.
    A visit next day found Ed feeling less chipper. Curling, Gra-
ham, Wolf, Stradikopulos, and Owen went over with me a third
time. We found the room empty. Making inquiry, we received
the shrugging information from a French Sister: "Mahonee,
parti." I wrote a note to Mrs. Mahoney from a dingy hotel
lobby. "Harold" had been evacuated to some base hospital and
I would let her know its location later. Joining the group who
had come with me, the six of us watched the drunken antics
of a small group of doughboys. The odor of cheap wine and
cigarette smoke filled the hostelry. Men made raucous, loudmouthed advances toward a tawdry group of camp-following
women. Graham thought he'd hang around for awhile. The
rest of us climbed the steep hill to our Deneuvre billets.
    It was raining in torrents when the battalion pulled out of
Deneuvre, according to sudden orders. The streets of Baccarat,
in the late afternoon, were flooded. The Neufmaisons road,
under a steady downpour, passed under tramping hobnails. It
wasn't so easy to "pick 'em up and put 'em down" in that direction as it had been when we were leaving the trenches. We
made Pexonne with difficulty and splashed off to the right,
accompanied by the familiar swish of artillery. A series of
winding hills through the downpour brought us floundering

and weary into a stretch of dripping woods. Platoons finally landed in a group of dark barracks. Rain splattered dismally on the metal roofs. Officers groped for nearby huts and fell into their musty interiors. A "sulphur dial" said that it was nine o'clock.[6]

Details splashed and slid to the foot of an inky hill to meet the kitchens. They rolled in at 1:00 a.m. and got stuck in a muddy ravine at the bottom. A wretched, soaking crew sat up on the hut floors until daybreak.

Morning brought a continuation of rain and new scenery. Camp de Ker Avor was in a dense forest. We were east of Pexonne and about three kilometers behind Badonviller. Skies cleared for a moment. A runner from Pexonne described an ephemeral rainbow that he had seen upon leaving the village for our bivouac. The incident was symbolic to many. The division was taking over the trenches of the Baccarat sector. Why shouldn't our insignia grace the heavens?

There was a bustle of work again. Kitchens were pulled up from the ravine in a drizzling rain. Husky men lent strong backs to help the quivering animals. Others with ropes to wagon tongues "heaved-ho" with grunting assistance. Slum and coffee were gulped in great quantity around noon among a swarm of Frenchmen. They splashed out of the forest soon after, leaving K and L companies and a detail from the sanitary detail, with a battalion of Italian woodchoppers.

We began to get settled in the sticky, dripping bivouac. Men were housed in wooden cantonments and officers spread their bedrolls in rustic huts that looked more attractive by day. K and L kitchens and officers' messes were combined for convenience. A small chapel stood near our billet. A narrow-gauged railroad wound through the woods to French batteries of 155 howitzers. The guns thumped away intermittently. Enemy shells dropped around distant Pexonne with muffled explosions. Apparently the forest was so vast that we were not to be bothered.

A surprise muster formation brought pay, now that we had no legitimate use for money. Bridge and crap games developed in the huts and more crap games took place in the barracks.

Officers, as usual, made up a pot of francs for the unfortunate Chink, who had no way of getting paid without a service record. Carling set up a barbershop and made a small fortune with scissors and clippers. French artillerymen, who manned the big guns, battered empty shell casings into ornamented vases. They ceased the work of art occasionally to remark, "Boches, pas bon!" They would follow this brief verdict with a few rounds of shells toward Germany and return to their profitable avocation.

We were as isolated as though we were on a desert island. Only rumors saved us from an oppressive ennui. Cherub turned up with a story about a second battalion officer named Quillian. The officer had gone to Maj. Stanton to plead for an assignment in the States. Quillian knew he was going to be killed, so the story went, and wanted to get out of the war. Men and officers, alike, greeted this gossip indignantly. "Th' yellow ————."

Chaplain Roberts came from nowhere and preached a sermon from the rustic pulpit to remind us that a week had seven days. News trickled in from the other units scattered around the area. An M company man had shot himself in the foot to get out of the misery. The body of an I company soldier, who had been missing for two weeks, was found in an abandoned trench, half-buried in the mud. He had evidently lost his way in the maze of trenches and been killed by shellfire. Ration carts came in from Neufmaisons with the news of two machine-gun battalion officers who had just been killed on the Pexonne road. They had been on horseback when hit and had died with the mangled animals.

Barney got hold of a map from somewhere and we began for the first time to take an interest in our location. We were in the Vosges mountains in the department of Meurthe and not far from the Swiss border. Places like Strasbourg, Mulhouse, and Metz were dots on the map fractions of inches distant. Lunéville, Nancy, and Toul were other map neighbors.

Rain continued to spatter all about us as we attacked a long-neglected mail sack of outgoing letters. Perce, Barney, Wally, Cherub, and I went to our job of censoring, glad for a relief from boredom. We chuckled heartily over some of the wild tales the boys wrote to the faraway homefolks. A letter, which Wally drew with a batch from the bottom of the sack, brought a tragic note to mingle with that of comedy. The letter from Russell had been written to his parents just before we had gone up for our first hitch in the trenches. We marveled over the prophetic contents of the pitiful message. The clean-cut Russell was sorry he had ever caused his father and mother any trouble and asked their forgiveness. He might be going into the lines any time and you never could tell—maybe he wouldn't come out again. All of us were deeply, if momentarily, affected. After a serious discussion, it was decided that the letter should be sent on as though nothing had happened.

Incoming mail brought welcome word from home and another terrible shock. I had just absorbed letters from June and the family; Barney had read messages from Capt. Gill and Lieut. MacNider, in Nice, and the latter's postscript, "Regards to Thompson and his night prowlers.—Hanford MacNider, Lieutenant, Ninth Infantry." What was it that Perce's baritone was saying? Mahoney? Well, what about Mahoney? Mahoney had died of gangrene in the Baccarat hospital, that's what about Mahoney. I couldn't believe it. I thought of the faraway mother in a panic. What had I done? The French nurse had tried to tell me that he was dead on that last visit—and I had thought she had meant he had been sent to another hospital. A frenzied letter of condolence went forward. I did everything I could with a pencil to explain the terrible mixup about "Harold." Men in my platoon barrack tried to console me. It was agreed that McDonough would write for all of the Sioux City fellows and explain my part to his friends, the Mahoneys. I could not sleep when we turned in. Ed's pathetic words repeated themselves over and over: "I'm gonna split Sioux City wide open."

A welcome sun streamed through the overhead foliage of Camp de Ker Avor. Mud underfoot was the only drawback remaining. The advent of replacements coincided with the war weather. L company drew Lieuts. Richards and Dorsey. The former was soon on his way again to other parts. Officers visited the platoon barracks to size up the new doughboys, who had come with the lieutenants. I drew nine of the new men. Three were Oklahomans. The other six spoke English as I spoke French—from a phrase book. Cpl. La Russo was a smart little Italian. The names of the others are enlightening—Privates Malatesta, Salvatore, Skurka, Chemilewski, and Zotos. I welcomed the pitiful newcomers outside of barracks with a fervent oration. I was their friend. That's what Uncle Sam had me there for. They relaxed and sighed audibly, understanding the "universal" language. Sergt. Bunce got busy right away teaching the group of foreigners how to get into their gas masks and how to load and unload their rifles. As Beavers remarked, the new men seemed to think that a Springfield was "somethin' to lean on."

A "memo" came through soon after ordering platoon commanders to dispatch one man each to division headquarters. The higher-ups were going to experiment with carrier pigeons for purposes of liaison. I immediately thought of Dupree, the half-wit. Here was a chance to kill two birds with one stone and perhaps a few pigeons along with them. I could place the imbecile in a safe place and at the same time be rid of a constant burden. Dupree did not respond to the new job happily. He was very sure that "he didn't wanta be no chambermaid to no pigeons." His plea to remain was so strong that I substituted Chemilewski, who seemed the most unlikely man of an unlikely lot. Chemilewski was palmed off on division headquarters with some misgivings, however. Maybe I had sent a good man instead of a poor one. A fellow just couldn't tell about men any more. Here were kids and sundry bums making fine soldiers and impressive-looking men making mediocre or sorry ones. Shy, reticent youths standing up to the job and former "hard-boiled eggs" turned softies. A few were running exactly true to all former estimations. Rich man, poor man, beggar man, and thief were reacting in a way to upset all kinds of peacetime values. The establishment of permanent patrol details and the selection of leaders knocked all of my former notions about men into a cocked hat. These men were selected for the special work of scouring no man's land, relieved of all other duties. It had been found that some officers were not daring enough. Others were daring without good judgment. Still others were willing, but lacked the necessary bump of location to prowl around in the night. Those officers chosen for the job had given indications that they had everything. I only had a speaking acquaintance with the patrol leaders of the first battalion, but I knew two of those in the second—the boy officer Wallace and the amazing "Frank Merriwell" Sawyer. What a shock it was to learn that an inveterate braggart could more than back up his high opinions of his own qualifications. If these surprises were not enough, Maj. Bronson finished the job by selecting Braddock, a fellow no one liked, and added the gawky, simple-appearing Cullen and the baby-faced Cherub. I never got over the sight of Cherub commanding a bunch of hard-looking men who followed him around as though he was Napoleon. To add to the strange picture he was perfectly natural and never seemed to be anything except the giggling kid he had always been.

Our patrol group made ready for its new duties. Tim came over unexpectedly to bid me good-bye. K company was off for Badonviller, leaving us alone with the Italians.

A matter involving the artillerymen who had come over with the regiment now occupied our attention. They had been separated from their outfit by an epidemic of scarlet fever, which caught them out on leave in the faraway days of Mineola. All platoon commanders were now ordered to return these men to their regiment, which was one of those that thumped away from the neighborhood of Pexonne. The artillerymen were sorry to leave us, now that they were firmly rooted. This was especially true of the low-browed Chink. We were greatly surprised when McDonough returned to the bivouac with Chink after taking him off with the others. A captain of artillery in a distant quarry had refused to take Chink without a service record. According to my sergeant, the artillery officer had taken one look at the grimy Landers and had added "with a service record" to his other objection. We all admitted that Chink was not impressive. There was some talk of attempting a compulsory scrubbing and trying the artillery officer again. In the midst of all of this Chink broke down and confessed everything. He had been afraid to say anything before. Something he had heard in Neufmaisons had led him to believe that he had gotten mixed up with a deserter. Chink wasn't even in the army, he related to a pop-eyed group of officers outside our hut. Perce's foghorned guffaws were accompanied by hearty laughter from everybody. Chink repeated his astounding assertion. He wasn't in the army. "Wasn't in th' army? Well, if he wasn't in th' army Perce Langworthy was shucking corn in Pottowatomie County, Iowa." The rather inarticulate Chink continued his story haltingly. He had been drunk in a Mineola roadhouse way back there in the fall when a soldier had offered him $5 to swap his "cits" for the soldier's uniform.[7] Chink wasn't so drunk that he did not know that $5 was $5. The next thing he knew those M.P.'s who raided the joint had dragged him protesting to Camp Mills, along with the others. Something said had been about scarlet fever and he had been bundled off to some other part of the darkness. When he had come to next day he had tried to explain things to Sergt. Runyan. Well, things just hadn't panned out, that was all, and Chink had found himself in the hold of the *President Grant* with all the rest of the seasick doughboys. That was Chink's story, and he stuck to it. Now that he was a "character" the men in the company began to treat him with a little more respect. His case was taken up with headquarters, but apparently the throne had other things to think about. There was no place else for Chink to go and he became a permanent part of us and a source of much amusement. Thus it was that a mystified "second looey" went back to the trenches with a bunch of "100 percent Americans," a scattering of one-tenth of 1 percenters, and a lone, unofficial ambassador of Uncle Samuel.

CHAPTER EIGHT

Badonviller

The loop of ditches called GC9 was the old familiar mudhole, with a few exceptions. A welcome sun that made life a bit more comfortable than formerly also accentuated the sewer-like odors of my dripping, rat-infested shelter and an adjoining sump-hole latrine.

Jensen now guarded the entrance to the deep sap, where men snored in lousy bunks after a wakeful night in the moonlit trenches. Others "sawed gourds" in the shadowy berths of my damp headquarters. Two outposts scanned the horizon of mud and wire while Collard lay on top of the shelter where Russell had met his death.

Liaison patrols and runners kept us in touch with Barney at PA5 and with our isolated neighbors, Dorsey, the new officer, and his gang in GC10, Sgt. Bunce and a gun crew at the farmhouse outpost. Perce commanded the left half of the company sector from PA6, with Sgt. Green and Wally in charge of the other front-line quagmires. Half platoons manned the strong points now that we had to cover more territory. I company had taken over the old French sector to the right; M and K supported the front-line troops from Badonviller and its kilometer-distant neighbor, Village Negre. Stokes mortars from Maryland, Hotchkiss machine gunners from Georgia and Pennsylvania, and other auxiliary units had relieved similar outfits, who now enjoyed a vacation in the world of rest.

A volley of Boche whiz-bangs brought sleepy men out of the shallow dugouts and into the trench bottoms before we were well settled. The flashing and banging caused the old fear to well up again, but the strafing ceased, leaving us coughing in the clouds of acrid smoke. We fell into the trench routine with a hangover of taut nerves and fearful expectancy. That night I splashed from outpost to outpost, with Owen at my heels.

Cursing half-whispers in the silver light disclosed that a snooping colonel had dropped down from nowhere to visit all posts ahead of me. A man on each post had been ordered to turn his rifle over to the officer, who demanded to see if the Springfields were properly loaded. Wherever the prowling officer had been able to secure a gun, he had promptly bawled out the culprit for giving up his firearm. There seemed to be no need for instructions on my part—Gen. Pershing wouldn't get the guns next time. Besides, if "that ———— of an inspector showed his lousy head again, he was gonna be lugged out of them ditches feet first."

Owen and I returned to the shelter to learn from McDonough that Col. McGinnis had just departed with hell in his bosom, or that part of Hades especially reserved for a certain second "looey" who was responsible for his men's shortcomings. I had started another round of posts, with my redheaded bodyguard, when a rocket shot heavenward from Dorsey's position. Six red stars popped into a spray, looped down gracefully, and were followed by an avalanche of whiz-bangs. Men scurried about amid the thundering noise, nervously demanding: "What th' hell?" Panicky groups slipped and slid along the duckboards to the alert positions in the fire trench. Stokes mortars in our rear and chattering machine guns joined the maelstrom which was tearing up the moonlit wire. The show continued for some minutes and then ceased abruptly. Imaginary Boches infested the moonlight ahead. Trembling doughboys "stood to" through a night of suspense and into an eerie dawn.

Liaison patrol brought enlightenment just before breakfast. Col. McGinnis, "th' ———— fool," had played the devil. He had ordered Dorsey in GC1 to send up a rocket to see if the artillery was on the job. Dorsey had demurred, trying to explain that telephones were used to get a test barrage of one shot. The colonel had delivered a picturesque lecture on the subject of insubordination, causing the intimidated lieutenant to let 'em have it. The colonel had then demanded, during the resulting volcano, that Dorsey have the barrage stopped and had been dumbfounded to learn that no one could halt the whiz-bangs once the signal for a barrage had been given. The pestiferous inspector now left the ditches, threatening Dorsey with court-martial.

Chow details struggling up from town with their heavy containers of slum pictured Maj. Bronson as foaming at the mouth and higher-ups of our supporting artillery as tearing their hair. The doughty colonel had given away their barrage lines and gun positions by his parade-ground antics.

Warm days were welcome but ghostly, moonlight nights were still made for overcoats. Owen and I made our difficult way from post to post, passing again and again the haunting scene where we had clipped the identification tags from the mutilated Marshall. We floundered through silvery bayous that had received the flying, shell-seared flesh of poor Russell. Hissing demands for the daily password from half-hidden sentinels brought spasms of goose pimples. Dawns came up with a waking world of reverberating rifle fire; I "stood to" in a fire trench, surrounded by Jensen, Stradikopulos, Wolf, Chink, Price, Gross, Ackerman, and my righthand man, McDonough. The new days, creeping forth, the gray expanse of mud and wire, filled a fellow's muddled brain with strange images, images of faraway home, of everything, of nothing; of the dead sentinel, whose ruddy face, never found, seemed to eavesdrop upon the silent groups who stared tired-eyed into the waste of desolation. Tense nerves would become alive to suspicious noises and to the presence of imaginary enemies, then one would lapse into rambling thought again. Those Germans who stood like us, in muddy trenches beyond the barrier of wire, what kind of folks were they, anyway? Funny, there were only two days to find out; crawl over, never to return, or travel clear around the earth and slip upon them from behind.

The hitch became wearing. Inspectors seemed to delight in visiting us soon after breakfast, during the only available moments for sleeping. One of these officers introduced himself as Capt. Underwood and mentioned Alabama. A reference to Chattanooga and we were swapping notes about the captain's University of Virginia mates, Burkett Miller and Ed Finlay, from home.

It was queer the way gossamer threads of the dream world of home wove themselves around our mudhole. Stowers, my gas guard, talked between nightly chores, in our dripping candlelit shelter, of a former career as a "barker" in a traveling carnival. The ludicrous bantam had seen the world and could prove it. He convinced me "toot sweet" with word pictures of Cleveland, Etowah, Rome, and Cartersville. Sure, he had "drifted" all through "th' wool-hat" country. "Why some uv them Tennessee hillbillies 'ud cut your throat for a ham sandwich." Had I ever been to Calhoun, Georgia? Well, they had a cigar store Indian down there, "settin' on a hunk uv granite." In a field, right along in there somewhere, the Eureka shows used to set up the big top. "Say, 'Loot,' whatever come uv th' deaf an' dumb black boy that used to meet all rattlers in Dalton?"

Nothing was happening, thank God, but I was usually tense with expectancy. Cherub, Braddock, and Cullen, sometimes accompanied by Sawyer, crawled out each night with patrols. Everybody was on the qui vive until pistol shot or flare signals from other parts of the moonlight announced their safe homecoming. Propaganda leaflets denouncing Hindenburg, the Kaiser, and crown prince must be fired into the old German trench opposite with a Very pistol.[1] Eaton and Woods, sent to Badonviller with excruciating rheumatism, and Salvatore was lugged back with a bad case of trench foot.

A laugh was worth a million dollars. At chow time Stowers elaborated upon a story going the rounds of "grapevine telegraph." An old, peg-legged German rode up and down the enemy trenches on a bicycle, equipped with flares and gunnery. A few shots, a flare from strategic points in the moonlight, created the illusion of many Boches. Imaginative slum toters reported a conglomeration of gossip about spies, Boche atrocities, a black dog that had been seen roaming our sector, and captured German women, wearing uniforms. Stowers was equal to all occasions, with appropriate comebacks. The joke was on me when I asked my gas guard facetiously, one raw and foggy morning, which he would rather have, a Croix de Guerre or a bottle of cognac. Muddy men, suffered at the response, delivered with feigned seriousness: "Loots sure could ask some dam' fool questions; they were worse'n inspectors." Owen, Chink, Collard, and Beavers, even Skurka and Zotos, who understood little English, went into convulsions when the clown demanded with a pantomime of mock severity, "Where th' hell is 'at giggle water?"

Shells swished, rifle fire cracked. A platoon of K company under Turk splashed up one morning to be greeted like long lost brothers. We filed through the ditches to Badonviller and piled into the cellars of the ruined town, where men heaved sighs of satisfaction.

"Phew! K can have them tronshays, fer all I care."[2]

"Boy, mebbe I ain't gonna git me beaucoo shut-eye!"

Our old hangout at "61" Grande Rue was inhabited by doughboys and cooties. Wally and I shared the cellar with Sgts. McDonough and Bunce, Cpl. Hazen, and Pvts. Stowers, Owen, Blair, Stacy, and Malatesta. The rest of the L family were scattered along the wrecked street and around the corner in the battered Rue Gambetta. The town was also populated with battalion headquarters, part of the sanitary detachment, engineer troops from California and South Carolina, and sundry patrol units. French troops were on the right of our new sector, with Alabama men of the 167th Regiment on the left. The artillery from Illinois, Indiana, and Minnesota, the units from New York, Ohio, Texas, and Oklahoma, made up a world that we knew only by sound or hearsay.

We fell into the old routine again. Guard details were established. The sleepy men and officers were up before dawn for "stand to" in the streets. Breakfast chow was followed by work details in the trenches. One of these jobs took me with a crew to PA6 and GC12. We splashed out by a machine gun, set up

behind a curtain of gunny sacking. GC12 was a veritable quagmire. Summary court prisoners, condemned to the front lines
permanently, for punishment, labored with picks and shovels
in the trench bottoms. A sausage balloon floated over the German rear area.[3] John Talbot, in command of the strong point,
was splattered with mud to the waist, but clean shaven and
natty from his pistol belt up. Habits of an innate refinement,
which I had thoughtlessly mistaken for old-maidishness on my
first acquaintance, could not be downed by all the slime. It
didn't seem real that such a genteel fellow was taking the
hardships and the dangers all in his stride, when the impos-
ing Clifton and the rough and tumble McCarthy had blown up
at their first glimpse of war. But curious lessons had been
soaking into my immature thinking apparatus ever since we
had come to the front. Fellows were neither "softies" because
they were fastidious, "goody-goody" because of strict personal
codes, dependable or unreliable because they thought well of
themselves, nor brave or cautious just because they seemed
tough.

I found Tim in a lousy bunk at the K company shelter. We
had passed like ships in the night, as he had gone up with K
and as I had come out with L. He grunted a weary "howdy,"
struggled out of a pair of slimy boots, and hit the hay for a
morning snooze. Capt. Allen, usually so full of life, seemed to
be feeling the strain, was very irritable, and so I did not tarry.

Back in town, the air was filled with talk of spies and snip-
ers. A few men of the second battalion had been wounded in
a peculiar manner, apparently shot from points in their rear.
A handful of old French men and women, who shambled
about the ruins with gas masks, were packed into carts forth-
with. Meager belongings were piled in also and the old people
rolled out of town with gesticulating protests, leaving
Badonviller alone with the Americans.

Life was relatively easy in the shell-scarred village. The
cellars of heavy stone were safe, and gas alarms caused the
use of suffocating masks only at infrequent intervals. We had
long since learned to judge the target of shells by ear. Those
that screamed meant a hurried duck to safety—or havoc.

Those that whistled usually brought buzzing fragments that made a fellow glad for his tin hat. The projectiles of the swishing variety were high above and headed for our supporting guns.

We worked, loafed, slept, and explored the ruins around us in this atmosphere of intermittent artillery. Two hikes throughout Grande Rue by daylight and two night reliefs had not permitted much knowledge of Badonviller. We proceeded between chores to the job of sightseeing.

A pottery on the way to PA6, with a gaping hole in its chimney, was a mass of half walls, scattered bricks, and smashed china. Wickland found a piece of broken saucer with a familiar trademark stamped on its bottom. Why, he had seen the insignia in his father's store in Keokuk. The souvenir was dispatched "toot sweet," to let his homefolks know where we were without running afoul of censorship.

A demolished Hôtel de Ville stood at the head of the Rue Gambetta. A dainty, untouched fountain nymph of bronze was surrounded by wrecked houses. Walls were smashed, plaster, broken shutters, and miscellaneous debris littered the street and sidewalks. The deserted dwellings, built flush with the walks, and the low stoops of stone were reminiscent of childhood visits to my grandparents in Maryland. Rue Gambetta might have been a smaller, more narrow Baltimore block after an earthquake. The ruins seemed haunted by departed spirits. It made a fellow wonder and wonder. What had become of the folks who had once loved, laughed, worked, and gossiped in Badonviller? How had they felt; what had they suffered in August 1914, when the Boches had swarmed in to sack the peaceful country?

A cemetery was stark with destruction. Iron gratings around mounds were twisted and torn; upturned graves, bombarded vaults, and scattered headstones finished the desolate picture.

A shell-torn and roofless church burned itself into my memory, its stone altar standing pathetically among crumbling walls. The interior was strewn with stained glass, broken pillars, and splintered timbers. Images of saints were pockmarked and wounded. A statue depicting the descent from the cross revealed a twice-murdered Jesus, whose limp body was supported by a hooded Mary. The crucified Saviour's arms were severed above the wrists and legs gaped from shell wounds.

A nine o'clock twilight settled over the Rue Gambetta. Barney, Wally, and I sat chatting in all that was left of a front-room library above Perce's cellar billet. Shelves of books were covered with mortar dust, while other volumes littered the dirty floor. Perce drowsed in a bedroll, spread upon an ancient table.

Our session of "raw chewing" was interrupted by footsteps in the street and the loud, cheery voice of our old pal, Sawyer. We went outside to find him and his small following with faces blackened like so many minstrels, in anticipation of a night patrol. The group carried grenades, pistols, and wicked trench knives; I felt sorry for unknown Germans. The big fellow passed the time of day and explained that Braddock, of our battalion, was learning the ropes of no man's land in front of the new sector and that he was going along to break the new patrol leader in. I asked Sawyer, jokingly, if he was coming back. It was not uncommon for a fellow to say, "See you later," and hear the joshing response, "Yeah, if one of us doesn't get bumped off first." I was surprised to learn that Frank Merriwell, of all people, did not appreciate the levity. His sooty face clouded as he accused me of being "a smart alec." The giant grabbed me in a bear hug and applied a painful hammerlock, half-mad, half-playful. He nearly threw me to the curb and departed with the pointed request that I keep my humor to myself in future. Coming so suddenly, leaving me no time for explanations, I was deeply mortified over the incident. The others had seen me manhandled in humiliating fashion and had laughed uncomfortably over the unpleasantness.

Men stood in the Rue Gambetta near the fountain next morning, talking with suppressed excitement. A shell swished over as I approached the group to hear the latest gossip.

I shoved my way into the circle of men and officers to have the war slap me in the face again in an overwhelmingly per-sonal manner. A few words from the talkers and I knew that

I would never be able to put myself right with Sawyer. Lunt and Ferns, of our company, who had been with him the night before, rehashed the confused details. Three officers and fifteen men had crawled out in front of GC7, had inched along on their bellies toward the extension of the old German trench that Cherub and I had once investigated. A man had been seized with a fit of coughing and Sawyer, who usually combined sensible caution with great daring, had offered the whispered suggestion that they call it a night. He had felt sure that the Boche had the patrol spotted. There were objections to this proposal from some of the others and the big fellow had then let it be known that he would go to hell with them, if that was the way they felt about it. The patrol had crawled through the night with painful difficulty. There had come a flare and a chattering burst of fire from a Maxim. Men had scattered frantically into shell holes. Groans of anguish had come from the darkness. McNaughton, one of the officers, found Sawyer, but was unable to move him. The wounded man had gasped that he was done for; he had been shot in the stomach and couldn't move his legs, owing to a probable injury to the spine. Frenzied efforts at rescue had followed, Sawyer groaning in agony at each attempt to move him. McNaughton had lain by the stricken figure for hours while others squirmed back through the night in search of anything that could be used for a stretcher. McNaughton had finally crawled back himself to round up help from the surrounding shell holes. A small group had made the site again just before dawn, but the huge figure was missing. A helmet and webbed belt lay where the group had last seen him; tracks in the mud seemed to indicate that the Germans had dragged off their prize roughly. Lunt and Ferns were sure that the patrol leader was fatally injured. They added, also, that Brooks, of K company, a member of the patrol, was missing.

Badonviller was cloaked in the pitch blackness of 2:30 A.M. Invisible, clicking hobnails mingled with the scraping feet of L company. A whistling shell banged down upon Grande Rue, demolishing a rolling kitchen. The night was filled with unseen commotion as wounded cooks were carted off in the darkness. Our kitchen was replaced by one just like it in the dim lantern light of a crumbling stable. The clomp-clomp of shadowy mules, the rattle of wheel on axle, gathered volume. Weary shuffling feet filed out of town into a wooded path and headed for the rest billets of Camp de Ker Avor. Artillery ca-rumped from a variety of distances and angles, as silent columns stumbled through the woods. It was tough—it was tough—to have to leave old Sawyer behind there in the melancholy darkness.

Forty-eight hours of undisturbed rest, a sponge bath, and a change of clothing made a fellow feel human again. Men shaved, washed clothes, scraped the mud off firearms and equipment around an ancient cistern. Others "read shirts" under the green foliage of the forest, where wild flowers blossomed in profusion.[4]

Perce was taken down with a severe attack of jaundice, but refused to go to the hospital. He got up instead, consumed a bottle of Prunella, and proceeded to make a shooting gallery of the Italian woodchoppers' kitchen. Brown figures, a well as those in gray-blue, scampered for the safety of tree trunks as tin cans and utensils plunked off a rustic counter. The invalid rid himself of another clip of "A5s" and called it a day. A good night's rest and our company commander was his normal self again.

Days were spent in loafing, roaming the woods, and writing and censoring letters. Another spell of moonlight found some of the K and L officers visiting back and forth between huts for sessions of gossip and poker. Maj. Bronson honored our shack one evening and it cost me sixty-seven francs to learn that he was a pretty good fellow and not one to be hated or feared. It was humiliating to recall that, while I had been consuming liquor, at first to be smart and later to relieve the sleepless tensions, I had condemned him for an occasional snort. It had not occurred to me before that the major was not as young as the rest of us, yet had to put up with much the same hard, grinding life.

Ration carts came in from the supply company at Neuf-maisons with news of the outside world. The wounded Van

had returned to duty with M. McCarthy, and a few other officers were to be sent back to the States. Runners brought other
meat for talk and gossip: a C company man had been killed by
shellfire in Grande Rue; an old Frenchman and his wife had
met a similar fate in Pexonne; four Boche planes had brought
down a French plane in flames beyond the village, while another enemy flyer had showered the town with leaflets of German propaganda. Gibbons rolled in with his supply of grub,
bringing a few samples of the literature. An inspection in my
platoon barracks revealed that all and sundry knew J. Pierpont
Morgan and Woodrow Wilson, two of the subjects of the Germans' ire. Some were not so sure about McAdoo, and Collard
wanted the dope on "this here" Baruch.[5] Sgt. Lawson tried to
explain from his store of knowledge but the unsatisfied
doughboy was laconic: "Never heard of 'im."

News of a deserting German who had wormed his way over
where the lines were close broke an ennui that was beginning
to pall, while Brooks, the missing K man, turned up with a
hair-raising story of his escape to our lines. He had lain in a
shell hole for a day and two nights, surrounded by Boches.
There was no news of Sawyer, and most everybody was convinced he was dead.

Men began to grumble over the enforced idleness, so close-
order drills up and down the mountain roads were started to
relieve the tedium. A bunch of foolish doughboys almost welcomed the prospect of action again. K pulled out one evening,
making life duller than ever with Tim, John, Turk, and "Cap"
Allen gone. We followed two days later for another eight-day
hitch in the trenches of the Baccarat sector.

CHAPTER NINE

The Last Trench Days

E ven a labyrinth of ditches can have its own distinct personality. GC12 offered a variety of vices and virtues. Birds twittered now and again in a scrawny apple tree behind my shelter of timbers and corrugated iron.

An ominous 155mm "dud" lay in the mud underneath the sparse verdure. Stryker labored from daylight to dusk on a suction pump to prevent seepage from flooding the low bunks in my underground headquarters. A lazy stream of muddy water poured from the mouth of a hose and into a ditch at the side entrance. Malodorous stenches came from a bayou latrine. A yellow blanket of buttercups, peeping from the wire that surrounded my half platoon, tried bravely to hide the raw brutality of shell holes and abandoned trenches.

The wreckage of a farmhouse stood in no man's land, halfway down a gentle slope from our fire trench. Rusty wire between and beyond met enemy barricades at the foot of the hill and spread out over a plain to a gaunt clump of woods, which hid the German trenches. The familiar sausage balloon floated against a blue May sky, behind the Boche positions. More rolling expanses of posts and crisscrossing rust hemmed in McDonough's invisible subsector to the left and covered the front of the adjoining Alabama sector beyond him. Indistinct trench tops to our right sloped down toward Wally's marooned crew in GC11. A suggestion of zigzagging parapets led on to

GC's 10 and 9, where Dorsey and Barney held forth, and disappeared into the shell-scarred woods beyond. Perce, in command at PA6, spoke through the medium of runners, chow details, written messages, and occasional tours of inspection.

A trio of enemy planes circled and droned overhead from time to time. An enemy sniper pinged away from the foot of the ravine in front of Wally's position. Gray-green ants crawled from the distant woods in front of us and scurried back "toot sweet" when my excited riflemen took potshots at the minute targets.

A chilly, sleepless night of eerie flares and cracking rifle fire gave way to a steady drizzle. Cherub and his gang of night prowlers crawled up from the misty blackness of the farmhouse ruins to be greeted by nervous half-whispers of recognition. The nightly patrols and vigils continued, flare and pistol-shot signals letting invisible friends know that the prowlers were home safely.

In the candlelit shelter, where rats scampered about and gnawed into our reserve rations of hardtack, Sergt. Lawson and I made daily reports of things seen and heard and greeted drawling liaison patrols from the Alabama sector. The Southerners couldn't be bothered with rifles; a grenade in the hand and another in an otherwise empty canteen cover was worth "beaucoo" small artillery. The boys from Alabam' did not think much of our passwords and countersigns, which battalion headquarters usually chose from French sources. Their own signals, sent us each day, were more original than "Côte d'Or and Bapaume;" "Toulouse and Grenoble," "Big-Boy," "Come sev'n–Come 'leben," "Little Phoebe," and other phrases from their stock of slang made a big hit with my bunch from the corn and hog country.

Summary court prisoners, who spent the long nights in Wally's deep sap, came over each morning with picks and shovels. They helped my men keep the strong point livable and commandeered sundry duckboarding from abandoned trenches near the ruined farmhouse. Deprived of all weapons as part of their punishment for past delinquencies, they seemed a heavy responsibility. I ignored the grenades, swiped from our ammunition dump and now bulging in their blouse pockets.

The sun shone again, bringing the balloon and the planes back with it. A brace of enemy shells banged into the ravine one morning and brown figures sprang out of the ground, as if by magic. Crawling, scurrying men stumbled through patches of wire toward us, to the tune of pinging bullets. Cherub, at the head of a panting crew, fell into our fire trench giggling nervously. The gang had been after the sniper. A bullet had seared the boy officer's back, wounding him slightly. The crowd splashed back to PA6, Cherub cursing his luck over a forthcoming shot of antitetanus.

Corpl. Blanton, at the outpost between us and McDonough, became panicky as the hitch proceeded and the contagion spread to his gun crew. When the rockets at my shelter entrance were missing, Lawson and I were more suspicious than ever of the noncom. The outpost was searched, the fireworks recovered, and Blanton sent to the company headquarters with his funk. I feared that I had done the corporal an injustice, but Lawson's judgment was quite consoling: "Better do him wrong than let him mess up the rest of the gang."

GC12 became overrun with visitors. Col. Townes floundered out and hobnobbed with everybody, with unaffected cordiality, while Maj. Winn, of the supporting machine gunners from Georgia, followed him. Inspectors came from division headquarters to have Lawson shake me out of a morning snooze and into my rubber boots for a round of foolish questions. Where was the nearest machine-gun position? How would I call for supporting artillery? What would I do if my command was suddenly surrounded by Germans?

The inspectors gone, I waded back to my dirty bunk amid the snores of Beavers and Owen. Stryker, on the suction pump, squirted tobacco juice into the muddy water and commiserated with me over the trials and tribulations of a "second looey." He'd like to slip a live "kernade" in one of "them inspectors' pockets." He knew what "them guys 'ud do if the Boches turned up—tear down a helluva lot uv rear wire!"

A British major general and his staff paid us a surprise visit and asked reasonable questions. The "high-muckety-muck," who looked younger than Perce, visited posts and talked to everybody in democratic fashion. A major with him said that the young general had started as a Tommy in '14. The visitors departed, leaving sundry doughboys wondering why our own inspectors couldn't act more like human beings.

Uneventful, half-expectant monotony, and sleeplessness began to pall until someone found a batch of Red Cross and Y.M.C.A. stationery in a crevice of one of the platoon saps. A job of letter censoring was added to the nightly chores. Our "nice cool sewer," as Stryker called it, was swamped with home-going literature. Lawson helped me with the missives, which were overly welcome. Envelopes were filled with buttercups, picked at arms' length from our parapets. Beautiful romances were woven around the dainty souvenirs. Messages revealed that the flowers were gathered from no man's land, while the writers were under machine-gun fire. One "true confession" stated that the scribbler had been rudely interrupted by a German patrol, in the midst of nosegay picking. More romance was developed from the hodgepodge of gossip brought by chow details. An observer in the rear, with field glasses, had sighted a woman entering a roadside dugout, behind the German front. The frau or fraulein became the martyred heroine of sidesplitting plots. Mills had run across her while on patrol. When Black saw her in no man's land she had on a German uniform, while Davis recorded that she had been captured on a raid into the Boche trenches. Williams capped the climax in a realistic pencil scrawl to "Dear Uncle Eph" in the faraway corn country. "Me an' th' loot an' Pooch Collard and a bunch" had found the dame chained to a "krauthead" machine gun. Uncle Eph's modest nephew added the reluctant detail, "I didn't like her looks none, so I give her a bayonet in the middle."

Was it five days and nights or five weeks that we had manned the ditches of GC12? Five weeks seemed more in accord with reality. Collard and Cross were seized with violent fits of retching. Jensen, Williams, and several others followed suit, throwing up the greasy slum a few minutes after the panting chow details had called "come an' get it." Liaison patrols reported that nothing of the sort was going on among our neighbors. I dispatched a message to Perce by my redheaded shadow, Owen. Wickland, Chink, and I had joined the procession when Maj. Branch, of the sanitary detachment, came up for an investigation. I was ordered to have the evil-smelling latrines filled up and a new one dug "toot sweet." My gang and the summary court prisoners got busy immediately with picks and shovels. Boche planes flew over and the digging was halted. Maj. Branch floundered up again and raised the devil over our slow progress. Grunting, sweating men labored for an hour only to dig into an ancient latrine site, filled up by former dwellers. Other places were tried and other deposits of mud and human offal uncovered. Maj. Branch became impatient. McDonough, on the left, sent messages of warning by a runner, "Boche balloon's got you spotted—we can see you digging from over here."

A fifth excavation brought the same result as the others. Perspiring men cursed the life of a doughboy. Disgusted, I gave them the choice of finishing the job or starting over elsewhere. Picks and shovels flew, in acceptance of the first alternative.

A runner came up with exciting news to push stenches and nausea into the background. Brooks, the K company man, who had made a hair-raising escape after the Sawyer patrol, had reported something for the higher-ups to think about. He had lain in a shell hole back of the German first line, surrounded by Boches, who labored mysteriously with picks, shovels, saws, and lumber. "Grapevine telegraph" also had it that Germans deserting in front of GC's 5 and 6, where the lines were close to each other, had verified the enemy antics. The Indiana batteries of 155's were going to break up the "krautheads'" playhouse, beginning at dusk.

Lawson and I got rid of the summary court prisoners and a supper chow detail, as the men piled into the alert positions for another sleepless night.

Friendly shells whizzed and swished over us, from the sunset to the left, and boomed into the woods on the right of the battalion sector. The heavies were almost on line with us, due to the curvature of the front. Men tried to keep their eyes on the falling dusk ahead, while the shells came on in a stream of enfilade fire.[1] The show was getting interesting. Coveys of thumping, banging projectiles alternated with red rockets from the woods, off and on through the night. More rockets in seemingly frantic succession and we were wide awake with excitement. "By God, them G.I. cans is fallin' short!—somebody's catching hell from th' Indiana guns!"

The shelling ceased for awhile and began again before dawn. A stream of fireworks verified our belief that the heavies were still falling behind our own lines. We left the trench wearily and Stryker took up his tobacco-chewing job on the pump with the worried observation, "Boy, them babies is beaucoo potent!"

Lawson and I, on needles and pins, and sleepless, got the small day crew settled. Tired doughboys gulped chow to the tune of our admonitions: "If we get shelled get out of the saps and into the trenches. . . ."

Nervous banter filled the ditches when the men scattered for a morning sleep. A pair joshed Wickland near the latrine in passing. If he got bumped off he sure would make good fertilizer for the buttercups. Wickland was in the midst of an appropriate rejoinder when a brace of German 77's banged into the farmhouse ruins. Another screaming eruption followed in the communicating trench to PA6. A third volley fell into abandoned trenches behind the ammunition dump. Scampering men hunted the trench bottoms with their bellies. The screaming, banging express trains came on in volume. Lawson and I stumbled over each other into a cloud of acrid smoke. My insides fluttered. There were visions of the mangled Russell— "My God!" The shells were whizzing at rapid intervals. The flattened Lawson hugged a pocket-sized prayer book and coughed apologetically in the smoke, "My sister give it—"

"Whiz-z-z-z-z-bang!"

We were showered with falling mud. Shells ca-rumped all around us. For minutes, hours, we huddled, cringing together on our bellies. A "dud" screamed with a thump into the mud behind us.

"Whiz-z-z-z-bang!—Bang!—Bang!" It was all over.

We struggled to our shaky feet. My knees misbehaved and I was still weak in the middle. We suddenly remembered the others. A slipping, sliding checkup followed in the battered ditches. Over a cave-in we found Eaton and Perry in the trench bottom gasping for breath. Perry explained that the concussion of a shell had knocked them off their gun perch.

We panted on beyond the pair. All was well at the left. "Thank God!" I muttered as familiar faces flashed near the latrine and the apple tree. Excited talk mingled with our scurrying feet when we headed for the right. We climbed over another cave-in. Smoke floated over a demolished gun-crew shelter. My heart went heavy like a brick. A chicken-wire gate, a mangled Chauchat rifle, and splintered duckboarding were scattered in a confusion of debris. The cloud lifted. Mills cringed against a bank, his head jerking in quick spasms, Dupree slobbered in the trench bottom with an awful palsy. The jerking Mills pointed toward the wreckage and stuttered, "Sh-h-h-." That was as far as he could get with his description of what had happened. Dupree blubbered, moaned, and shook horribly. I seemed to be shaking inwardly, in unison.

Stowers and Collard floundered up and went hurriedly for litters. The Greek came back with them and helped Mills to PA6. I stood by speechless as poor Mills stumbled off, his head still jerking. I swallowed a succession of lumps when Stowers and his buddy labored off, sweating, with the fellow who didn't want to be a chambermaid to the carrier pigeons.

Men were gesticulating in description of personal miracles, when Lawson and I made the shelter entrance. Smith, a runner from McDonough, came up the trench with a routine message—"200 77's in GC12 and vicinity from 7:20 to 7:40 A.M.—Got by light over here."

We splashed inside the shelter as Chink and Owen waded in through the side entrance, still exclaiming over their narrow escape. We chattered loudly in a hangover of hysteria. A rasping snore and a snort came from one of the shadowy bunks. Beavers came to from a dead sleep and hopped into the ankle-deep water in his stocking feet. He slipped, fell, looked wildly about him and demanded, "Whasa matter, huh? Whasa matter?" We laughed with raucous abandon and felt better to learn that the soaking corporal had slept peacefully through the bombardment.

There was no more rest for the weary. Runners began to trickle in with news of our neighbors. GC's 11, 10, and 9, and PA5, had been strafed at the same time we got ours, but there were no other casualties in L.

Shells fell into the farmhouse ruins off and on all day to fill us with spasms of passing dread. A liaison patrol brought word of M company casualties of the night and of the strafing by our own 155's after daybreak. A 155 had fallen short, strafing the side of a platoon shelter where men were just turning in. A cave-in had trapped the victims, rockets had caught on fire, and the shelter consumed by flames. Rescue gangs from the company headquarters had worked frantically with picks and shovels to save the living, if any, but the angry flames had finally forced them to look, helplessly, at the cremation. An officer, a sergeant, and a private had been killed and another private fatally wounded. A fifth man was wounded slightly, while another was badly burned, but escaped miraculously when the concussion had blown him through a rear entrance to the shelter.

We waited in isolation until late afternoon for the full details and an account of other casualties. The heavies had fallen short in Village Negre, killing an I company corporal and mangling the first sergeant and three privates. The other tragedy had taken place in GC5. Several of the men were known to some of mine and all of them knew Sergt. Holm of M.

I was leaving the shelter for "stand to" when a voice in the dusk finished the details. "The 'loot' that got bumped off sure was a swell little guy," the stranger was saying. I was dazed and unable to take it in, when the voice continued, in answer to the question of Lawson: "No, sir, they don't make 'em better'n McLemore!"

A long night emerged into another clear day. The summary court prisoners sweated along with my bunch in repairing the effects of the shelling. Young, whom I had not seen since

Rimaucourt, came out with a "one-pounder" and crew to bang away at the site of the supposed sniper. We spoke of poor Mack and recalled intimate happenings of the faraway past.

Perce splashed up with the joyful news that we were to be relieved at dusk. We were going to Neufmaisons and into real houses again. Beavers was detailed to go ahead and arrange for billets.

Lieut. Creston and a half-platoon of H company were as welcome as so many Santa Clauses when they splashed up at the end of the lengthy day. A commotion of rifle fire and grenades cracked and boomed in Wally's direction while H was taking over our fire trenches and shelters. We staggered through the winding trench to the machine-gun position and passed "the dark outline" of the demolished pottery. It was dark when tired, scraping feet stumbled through Grande Rue and took the Pexonne road for the seven kilometer hike to billets.

Myriad invisible hobnails scraped with our own in the dark streets of Neufmaisons. A familiar voice greeted us at a dark corner and men fell wearily into sundry dark stables. Beavers led Lawson, Owen, Wicklund, and me to a shadowy dwelling, where we tumbled into the candlelight of two adjoining rooms. The heavy figures of Barney, Dorsey, and McCarter amid a group grunted feeble greetings and made themselves ready for bed in a confusion of muddy equipment. It seemed a month since we had been together.

Perce sat tailor fashion in his bedroll, rubbing a pair of swollen feet and imbibing drams of Prunella. When Wally and his crew staggered in an hour later, most of us were groggy. I lolled in delicious relaxation after the sleepless stretch in the trenches. Wally struggled out of his pistol belt and heavy hobnails. Blair dumped a Boche helmet and a pair of dark leather leggings in a candlelit corner with the irritable comment, "Them H company's—wanted to hog everything—said th' tronshays belonged to them when it happened."

"When what happened?" Perce demanded, thickly. Wally gave a tired description of the melee that had developed during the relief. A large Boche patrol had raided an outpost in

GC11 and one Boche had been cornered like a rat in the ditches. He had been killed after putting up a magnificent battle. Wally was sure that doughboy bombs and rifles had cornered others in the wire.

Tired, nerve-taut men crawled out of their bunks for more Prunella. The habit of sleep seemed to have become a lost art. Wally and Blair kept on with the gory details, but I was too delightfully drunk to take it all in. Instead, my muddled brain played with the strange idea that such a serious, conscientious fellow as Wally should be mixed up in a killing. It meant little when the pair recounted the details of how an H company man had been knocked out with the butt of a Boche gun. I digested the cold facts without accompanying emotions when they explained that a "potato-masher" grenade, hurled by one of the Boche, had mangled another doughboy named Easton.

The dead German was a noncom, Blair recorded, while Wyche and Hosely agreed that the slain enemy was "plenty tough."

The groggy crowd swapped thick-tongued notes on the melee and on the eight-day grind just over. Perce fondled the German's ample leggings and indulged a picturesque admiration over the whole affair. He wrapped one of the puttees around a skinny shank, as Wally crawled into his bedroll. A muscle bulge in the black leather calf brought forth other expletives from Perce. "Huh," he grunted in interrogation, "he musta been a big hombre, Wally?" but a sprawling Wally snored loudly in his pallet of wrinkled blankets.

CHAPTER TEN

Paradise

eufmaisons was a town of hot and dusty streets, of primitive houses and barns, of smelly cafés and neat piles of manure. Neufmaisons was a medley of farm wagons, horse troughs, poultry, animals, soldiers, and peasants. Neufmaisons was divided into halves by an open-air sewer of masonry, whose odors seemed no sweeter because of the poetic name, Ruisseau de la Verdurette. Neufmaisons was a veritable paradise.

A group of Y.M.C.A. workers, whose hut was set up in a shambling stable, a scattering of French infantrymen, a detail of tolerant M.P.'s, and a recently deloused mob of New Yorkers and Iowans shared the glories of this heaven on earth.[1]

Disheveled men lolled under the shady eaves of the drab buildings. Others, in uniforms crimped into thousands of wrinkles by the delouser's dry steam laundry, tossed ball in the streets and barnyards. A few doughboys spent most of their waking hours in the pungent grog shops. Fewer still ogled and were wooed in turn by a handful of bedraggled women of doubtful age and certain avocation.

Mme. Peloubet, the untidy but hospitable hostess to Perce, Barney, Wally, Dorsey, and me, eagerly ladled out "des oeufs," "du vin," and omelettes from a meager larder, in return for precious francs. Madame was both pop-eyed and garrulous over our voracious appetites—"Américain, beaucoo monzhay! Beaucoo, beaucoo, beaucoo!" and the waddling old lady would

puff out her cheeks and stick out her roly-poly front in illustration of what was to happen to the skinny Perce if he didn't
cut down on the grub.

A motorcycle and sidecar sputtered up to our billets after
one of these joyful feasts. The family smoked and basked on
the stoop when the rider dismounted and asked for Lieut.
Malcolm. Our fellow looey answered with unfeigned curiosity.
The soldier saluted: "Sir, Gen. Browne sends his compliments
and requests the pleasure of Lieut. Malcolm's company at dinner." A flabbergasted Wally recovered somewhat, primped for
the party to the tune of brutal kidding, and rehearsed the late
Boche killing in GC11, for the sumptuous interview to follow.
He mounted the throne on wheels and left an open-mouthed
group coughing in a cloud of dust and burning oil.

Lusty voices and octaves from a feeble piano came from the
nearby "Y" hut. The song was new to us and catchy—

> K-k-k-ka-ty, bee-u-ti-ful Ka-ty,
> You're the only g-g-g-girl that I adore—

A contagion of new songs followed, going the rounds of
streets, cafés, and haylofts: "Keep Your Head Down Allemand,"
"Mademoiselle from Armentières," "Bon Soir, Ma Cherie," and
a host of others. A parody on one of Harry Lauder's favorite
hits had its day:

> Oh, it's roamin' in the gloamin,
> Out in no man's land.
> It's roamin' in th' gloamin',
> With a trench knife in your hand.
> When th' flares light up th' sky,
> An' you know it's time to die—
> Oh, it's lovely, roamin' in th' gloa-oa-oa-oa-
> min'.[2]

The dusty streets, swarming in the late twilight, with soldiers and elderly peasants, were filled with the strains of the
151st Field Artillery band. A cosmopolitan audience crowded

a barnyard square and lined its stone walls, enraptured by "Washington Post," "Madelon," "Beautiful Lady," and "Stars and Stripes Forever." Pig-tailed girls stared round-eyed or giggled at the hobnailed and blouseless flautists. Dirty-faced boys in smocks and horizon-blue trench caps peeped into the bell of the bass horn, aped the sliding trombones, and left the drummer little elbow room for his varied and fascinating duties.

There were a few flies in the ointment, of course. The intermittent thumping beyond the hill brought spasmodic reminders that paradise was a temporary affair. A few gestures of discipline were necessary to deceive snooping "bigwigs." A batch of raw replacements had to be initiated to the joys of "squads east and west" and to the tear gas fumes of a subterranean chamber, to get used to their masks. Salvatore and Blair and a handful of K men had to be shipped to the Baccarat hospital with raging trench fever. Tim must go to Pexonne, with his legal talents, to defend Gibson of my platoon, who faced a court-martial for an old offense. A scattering of gentlemen in brown had to be retrieved by their platoon commanders and sergeants from a stable guardhouse, after sleeping off the effects of "beaucoo" Prunella. There were a few cases where the retrieved in turn retrieved their retrievers among the enlisted men and noncoms. The officers usually threw their parties indoors and took care of their own delinquents. The M.P.'s seemed satisfied to see that Neufmaisons suffered no major calamity at the hands of the small number of real "tough hombres."

McCarter and Stowers, always an inseparable pair when war permitted, imbibed much, but carried the fluid as well as could be expected. They zigzagged toward me once, in the dusty Rue de Paris, and received the stern advice to beat it to billets, where they could be careful if not altogether good. The grizzled McCarter swayed unsteadily in the warm May breeze and eyed me with an amused gleam of animal cunning. Stowers, swamped in a pair of tent-like breeches, and with his trench cap cocked over a shaggy eyebrow, smeared me with a windmill salute and announced with blear-eyed solemnity, "A word to th' wise is sufficient." The pair staggered off to a round of hayloft jibes, reeled north and south at a horse trough, realized their mistake, and went around the obstruction arm in arm to allay a well-known superstition.

Mail brought a mixture of emotions into the life of lazy rest, letters from June and Dad were devoured. Newspapers of ancient vintage were scanned, but made little impression. Tim came over to compare notes and to bring a newsy letter from his sister, as was his wont. He received, in return, a sixty-day-old *Times,* containing a letter he had written to the homefolks many weeks before.[3]

I read and reread the mail from a world that seemed remote before attacking that from other points beyond the Atlantic. One of the latter got under my skin in a way to dampen the joy of all the others. It was from Mrs. Mahoney in faraway Sioux City and poured out a mother's grief. Why had I deceived them so about Harold's condition when I had written from his bedside in Baccarat? My encouraging word had been received one day and the official notice of Harold's death had come in a short time later. I had added a heavy weight to their sorrow by contributing to the terrific shock.

I slept little that night and was even bluer next day, when Tim, John, and the rest of the K crowd departed for Pexonne. Home and homefolks seemed indistinct, but Mrs. Mahoney had reached out across three thousand miles of space. Another batch of papers was accompanied by three more letters from the grief-stricken mother. Tears were mingled with tormenting insinuations. She had heard that officers let the men do all the dirty work. Where was I when Harold received his wounds? Why wasn't I with him? Would I write as soon as possible and let them know what I was doing when poor Harold went out to meet death?

A miserable "second looey" tried by pencil to explain the awful mixup to the faraway mother. So the war wasn't over just because a fellow was behind the lines. Misery grew to such proportions that I hiked all the way to Pexonne to see Ery, the intelligence officer. He'd have a copy of the patrol report covering that night in no man's land. I forgot all about censorship until Ery reminded me with blunt sympathy, "Why you dam' fool, you can't send that stuff home—forget it."

Back in Neufmaisons, Corpl. "Happy" Beavers, Private Bob
Wickland, and Private Weary O'Connor helped me to do so,
when they called on me in billets about a delicate matter.
Some of the New York Irish in neighboring stables had made
the cocksure claim that they could beat L company at baseball.
I had said something about being a catcher—how about helping get up a team?

Candidates were requested to meet after a retreat formation
and a group of doughboys gathered around. The lank O'Connor
had dug 'em out of the dirt around first base for Muscatine, in
a dreamlike past. Redding, a loose-limbed giant, was a pitcher
who admitted modestly that he had had "a cup of coffee" with
Des Moines of the Western League. Johnson, of Wally's platoon,
had shagged flies in the outfield at Grinnell College. Sandlotters
were chosen for other positions by a process of eliminating.
Boderick, one of our cooks, was commandeered from his job of
potato peeling when someone disclosed that he was a veteran
third sacker who held souvenir "pink slips" from Burlington,
Waterloo, and Moline. A mention of having piddled around with
the Chattanooga Lookouts for part of one spring and the "ex-
busher" asked if I had ever run across a lefthander named
Lorenzen who was down there for awhile. "Well, I'm a son of
a gun," I exclaimed, as I recalled the wild southpaw. Boderick
uttered an "I'm a son of a gun" on his own account and related,
"Him an' me was on th' club together at Ottumwa in '13."

The game took place next day, balls and gloves popping out
mysteriously from hayloft billets. A few bats, a mask, mitt, and
protector were supplied by the folks at the "Y." Players stripped
off their leggings and shirts. Batting and fielding practice proceeded while a field back of town filled up with troops and
natives of Neufmaisons and a battalion of the 165th Infantry
from a neighboring village. The gang of lusty fans began to
"get the mud off their lungs" from the moment a supply company sergeant announced the batteries: "For E company,
165th, Halloran and Maguire; for L company, 168th, Redding
and Thompson."

Money flashed, the fans cheered loudly and indulged in un-
printable repartee, as the Irish scored a run in the first inning

and as Redding breezed along after that, as though he had had
several cups of java with the Detroit Tigers. A circus catch by
Ferns in center, near the borderline of wheat, shut off a run in
the fourth. Another Irish threat was killed by a fast double play,
Semones to Beavers to O'Conner. We went into the last half of
the eighth still trailing, 1 to 0; the crowd went wild when we
filled the bases with two out on a single, an error, and a walk.
Johnson came up and poked one into the wheat for two bases,
Bradley Webber and I trotting home to the tune of cheers and
catcalls. In the ninth an Irishman grounded out, Semones to
O'Conner, while another flew out to Weber in left. The last
man swung grunting and missed a final, sweeping curve ball.

Doughboys swarmed all over the place, kidding and settling
bets. The players shook hands and made hurried arrange-
ments for a return game. The Irish fans went out of town, followed by raucous jeers, "If you see anything of Hank Gowdy,
over in the 166th, tell him to bring his gang of ball tossers over,
toot sweet."

The band played that evening and I hobnobbed with the
players of both teams in the crowded barnyard. I rolled into bed
with Barney and Wally a few hours later, in a contented frame
of mind. A group of revelers split the warm night outside:

> *An' when th' m-moon shines, over th' cow*
> *shed,*
> *I'll be waitin' by th' k-k-k-kitchen door.*

My bedfellows seemed to agree about paradise: "It's a good
war, boy; it's a good war, here in Neufmaisons."

Barney, Wally, and I drowsed in our bedrolls, undecided
whether to get up and eat or sleep some more and do without
grub until lunch. A commotion of voices and sputtering motors
in the street below made us choose the former course. We
were dressing when Owen turned up with the news that hell
had broken loose in the night. Talkative groups had gathered
when we got outside. Ambulances were rolling through town
in a dusty procession. News trickled in from a variety of
sources. The Boches had pulled a projector gas attack on Vil-

lage Negre. Sealed tins of liquid phosgene had been catapulted over by some unknown method, where the lines were close. Coming in batteries of tens and dozens the gas containers were accompanied by a heavy bombardment of the gassed sector and of Pexonne and Badonviller. A heavy toll of casualties had been taken from A, B, and C companies and a smaller number from K, M, and I, the sanitary detachment, the headquarters company, and auxiliary units.

Perce's bellowing voice interrupted our excited foray for all details. An order had come down for us to relieve the stricken survivors in the strange sector of Village Negre. "All right, gang, les' get goin'!" barked the energetic Perce.

Neufmaisons was a riot of frenzied activity. A bedlam developed in a scramble for equipment and a hurried rolling of packs. The company finally lined up for a rapid inspection. Perce barked commands as platoon commanders and noncoms made a final survey of squads, who stood at attention in "open ranks." Perce bellowed, "Inspection—arms." Two hundred-odd Springfields snapped to port, with a rattle of opening bolts and magazines. The command, "Order arms," brought a clicking of triggers and a startling shot. David, of Wally's platoon, fell out of ranks on his face. A new man in the rear rank had shot him by accident, while trying to remove a cartridge from the unfamiliar rifle. The dusty, groaning figure squirmed in agony with a broken hip, while Stacy hotfooted it across the verderette to get help from the sanitary detachment. A squad worked over the groaning figure. Men stood by awkward and helpless. A scurrying detail panted up with a litter. The litter, now heavy with David's shattered body, disappeared into the back of an ambulance as hobnails tromped by the horse trough. We raised a cloud of dust in the Rue de Paris, climbed the Neufmaisons hill, cut through the woods by Camp de Ker Avor, and hit a winding mountain road for Village Negre.

The following thirty-six hours in the unfamiliar sector left a mélange of indelible impressions.

A gang of haggard A company survivors stumbled out of a hilly, wooded area as we stumbled in. The swollen bodies of dead rats were strewn along a hard-surfaced road, which skirted the base of a steep ridge. The odor of dead life mingled with the sickening-sweet hangover of phosgene gas in a series of log dugouts and cubbyhole shelters, whose narrow entrances and sodded roofs, dotting the hillside, were suggestive of a community of "mound builders." Leaves and other sparse foliage were seared and yellow, as if by a killing frost. More rats and the twisted fragments of gas containers lay here and there in the steep, winding trenches, which led to GC's 5 and 6. The strong points, manned with miscellaneous troops and strange officers, looped along the reverse slope of the hill, their outposts extending over the crest into a maze of broken trees and wire. A gaunt stretch of rolling country sloped toward the French on the right and American positions on the left. The front was cut by a wooded ravine, beyond which the German parapets could be indistinctly seen one hundred yards away.

News of the recent attack had come to us through runners, liaison officers, the few remaining stretcher-bearers and auxiliary troops, and a detail from the sanitary attachment, which had replaced its counterpart in a system of underground chambers near our hut of logs and sod. The number of dead had run up to twenty-odd, while some one hundred-fifty other victims had been carted out of the positions we now occupied, out of Badonviller and Pexonne and out of our old trench positions a kilometer to our left.

Capt. Flood and Lieut. Green, of the machine-gun company, were dead of gas. Capt. Atkins, of A, was still alive, but his life was in doubt. Two Y.M.C.A. men had been killed on the road near our hut during the shelling that had come with the gas. Lieut. Riley, of the machine-gun company, who had been with me on the way from the French training school, was in the Baccarat hospital, condition undetermined, while Preston, who had come out with us, had collapsed in GC8 and was in the throes of bloody lung hemorrhages when stretcher-bearers had rushed him out of the ditches. The Boche had penetrated the old vulnerable spot of GC11 again, and hand-to-hand encounters had developed in front of GC's 8 and 9, while the blanket of vaporizing phosgene was descending upon Village Negre.

There was a moonlight night, during which we settled down in our shelters, a day of reconnaissance and a third mess of slum from a rolling kitchen, set up in the road. All was quiet in the candlelit dugout, but the moonlight outside seemed charged with electricity.

It was 10:00 p.m. L company was galvanized into action by a runner from Capt. Doss who commanded the battalion of mixed troops. The scrawled message said that the French intelligence had tapped the Boche phone lines somewhere along the stricken front and had eavesdropped on a conversation in German. A feeble voice had said that a raid on GC5 and 6 was to take place at 12:30 A.M. Other snatches of the conversation disclosed that a bombardment would precede the assault.

Perce bellowed instructions in the candlelit shelter. A detail was dispatched to BC6 to warn the officer there. Our company commander hurriedly repeated the password and countersign in effect among the neighboring French on the right and ordered me to check the warning in GC4, and to notify the troops in GC5, the Stokes mortars and machine gunners in their right rear, and a detachment of supporting infantrymen just above us. Barney, Wally, Dorsey, Runyan, McDonough, and groups of corporals scurried into the moonlight as Anderson and Brooke followed me into another part of the silvery night.

Anderson, Brooke, and I hurried to our duties in order to get through before the artillery fireworks should start. We passed the word to moonlit groups on the hill. Groping slowly through a dry, winding trench running into unfamiliar territory, we came into a loop of ditches, where a shadowy poilu led us to a candlelit shelter. Before I could finish a breathless warning in French phrase-book fashion, a dusty figure in horizon blue interrupted with gesticulations, "Si, si, mon lertna—Compree, compree." We headed off for GC5, Anderson observing with apparent truth, "These dam' Frogs know what th' krautheads are up to before they know it themselves."

An explosion in the wire off to our front and chattering machine guns brought us to the alert in a lonely strip of connecting trench. We progressed stealthily around the moonlit bayous, with firearms in hand. What if a pile of Boches should tumble into this isolated ditch? The thought brought goose pimples galore. We groped forward cautiously, stopping every few minutes to listen for suspicious noises. We made GC5 amid intermittent bursts of chattering, reverberating fire. Lieut. Wooster, whom we located in a fire trench surrounded by busy riflemen, received our ominous news with the half-whispered assertion that the Boches had blown up patches of wire in the wooded ravine we had just traversed. Wooster was in a stew. As long as I had to report back to Village Negre, would I hurry like hell and send him a couple of Chauchat rifle squads?

The three of us clambered off, half running down a steep communicating trench. We had been gone something like two hours by the time we neared Lieut. Miller's machine-gun post and its adjoining shelter. A terrific roar and a blinding flash split the heavens. We ran into the shelter as an avalanche of shells whistled into the woods. A tree bough fell back of us and dirt and gravel rolled off of the shallow dugout's roof.

A group of dim figures huddled against the walls inside. Miller's expression behind the flickering candle was wide-eyed. The crashing, roaring artillery filled the woods and the old nameless dread that I had known before returned. I wondered vaguely if my own shaky feelings were as apparent as Miller's. There was a dialogue between my two inner selves as the pounding continued. "Wooster needs help," one of these persons whispered. "To hell with Wooster," an inner devil replied, "You can't go out in that storm." There seemed to be a lull outside. An emotion that had nothing to do with a sense of duty welled up to help my fellow looey in GC5. The men in Miller's shallow dugout were strangers. Perce, Barney, Wally, McDonough, Stowers, Jensen, and the host of doughboys who made up the only family I knew were elsewhere. Something big was happening and I was overwhelmed by a desire to be with my own crowd. I rushed out of the shelter, against the protests of Miller, with Anderson and Brooke at my heels. The shelling grew voluminous again. Through blinding, deafening flashes we rattled down the duckboarding of a steep trench. We came out on the road, where white clouds of smoke floated low in the thundering moonlight. A flashing explosion threw me against a bank. I scrambled to my feet. Anderson and Brooks had disappeared as if by magic. I called to them in a shaky yell. The terrifying knowledge that I was alone pervaded my being. I ran down the road through the flashing thunder, stumbling, falling, and stumbling on again. A flash threw me flat as I neared the silvery outline of our shelters. I scrambled up frantically and ran into the haven of home.

The sight that greeted me, as I stared panting but transfixed into the dim candlelight, had the peculiar, unreal qualities of a slow-motion picture. Seconds seemed ages as I took it all in, forgetting the maelstrom outside. A bloody-faced and unrecognizable figure lay writhing and groaning on the floor. A pair of familiar legs lay just beyond the horrible sight. The sickening realization that the legs were Barney's was made more horrible by an expanse of gaping, bleeding flesh. But something was wrong with the gory scene. "What is it?" I wondered with anguish, my confused brain refusing to function. "My god! Barney's got on a mask." Another masked figure worked over him, as he tried to tear the respirator off. I tore into my mask in the frantic jiffy and immediately became blind. I was again conscious of the shelling outside and of a sickening sweet odor. Unseen hands pushed me onto a bunk. I vomited violently and tried to tear my mask off. Muffled admonitions were without avail. Someone was strangling me. Now rough hands were holding me down, while I vomited in the mask and bit into the rubber mouthpiece. I felt like a cornered rat. Eyes burned, nose clips pinched. An excruciating band of rubber was cutting into my forehead. The strange noise outside changed into a methodical series of thumps. Hours, hours. Strange shuffling movements. Muffled noises in the shelter. My temples throbbed. My inflamed imagination raced in a kaleidoscope of rational thought and lurid pictures. Nobody had on a mask on the hill. Was Barney dead? Was I going the way of Capt. Flood? Why hadn't Klaxons screamed a warning of gas? Who belonged to that awful smashed face? Wooster, Wooster! Who was Wooster? Barney, Barney, Barney! What was that strange, booming noise, noise, anyway?

Hours—hours. Suffocating ages. Quiet outside.

Feet scraped on the shelter floor. A foghorn voice was barking meaningless instructions. Someone pulled my mask off and I saw a dim figure through scalding tears. My throat was parched; my head pounded inside. The bleeding figures were gone. My sight improved. Dark pools stained the dusty floor. I slowly gathered my wits. I vomited at a whiff of musty-sweet gas. The dugout entrance made a rectangle of gray light. Feet scraped once more in an unseen part of the shelter. Familiar, spindly shanks in leather puttees were visible in the dugout floor. Just beyond was a figure on a litter coughing violently, near a rubber-tired wheel. The loud voice was barking again, "Shake it up, Wally, we gotta get these men out o' here."

CHAPTER ELEVEN

Hospital and Home

Vittel, a jewel-like resort of the Vosges, was no longer a playground for the continental rich. Its ornate Central Hotel, Nouvel Hotel, and other famous hostelries were now inhabited by gassed and wounded convalescents of the 42nd Division.

A few French and British were mixed in with the Americans. Patients clad in bathrobes basked upon the hotel balconies of grilled iron. Doughboys and artillerymen in shoddy, nondescript getups of brown, gray, and rusty blue hobbled on crutches in the peaceful parks, lolled upon the benches of a casino pavilion, and dotted a fairy-book town square of shops and cafés.

A former salon at the sumptuous Hôtel de Lorraine, now lined with hospital cots and frequently visited by nurses and women of the Red Cross, was filled with Rainbow officers evacuated from the Baccarat hospital three weeks before.

Barney, suffering tortures from his mutilated leg, which hung in a Balkan frame of ropes, pulleys, and heavy weights, occupied an adjoining alcove.[1] Division mates from the Ohio infantry, the Indiana field artillery, the Maryland trench mortars, the engineers, and a balloon corps officer with a broken arm were among those present. Riley, Silva, Varn, and Setliffe, of 168th, also had cots near my own, and like me seemed to be out of the woods. Capt. Atkins, of A company, old and haggard from the overdose of phosgene gas, still shambled about between treatments for his heart and lungs.

Turns at Barney's bedside, rambles through the parks, church on Sunday, visits to nearby Contrexéville with the others, made up my days. Between times we lived and relived the gas attacks, now swallowed up in four weeks of history. The whole thing had been a jumble of vivid scenes and lurid impressions. These had been very real when one was cornered with them, but some of the horror had been washed out by rest and absence from the front. I felt that a few miracles had happened, but was too glad for life to indulge in much deep meditation.

We had had little thought of gas as all of the talk of the night previous to the attack in Village Negre had been about an expected Boche raid. The raid had developed in unsuccessful assaults upon GC's 5 and 6, and more blood-spilling affairs in our old sector in front of Badonviller. Six or seven Americans and numbers of Boches had been killed in the fray.

No one had had on masks on the ridge above Village Negre or at Miller's machine-gun post, when the holocaust had struck. The suffocating L company in the low hollow had been trapped so suddenly that they had no chance to sound the klaxon alarms. Anderson, Brooke, and I had mistaken the gray gas clouds on the moonlit road for the usual residue from bursting shells. The excitement of it all probably deadened our senses of smell, while the gory sight which had confronted me in the candlelit shelter had set my brain in a muddled whirl. It never occurred to me that Hassler's bloody face was without a mask because of a horrible wound in the jaw. Nevertheless, I was into my own mask in a much shorter time than it had seemed.

Hassler had been hit outside and Barney had led a group into the thundering moonlight to rescue him. A shell fragment had taken a cross-section of bone and sinew out of Barney's thigh and both of the wounded men had been dragged into the shelter by the others. Nothing could be done for poor Hassler, while Barney had nearly bled to death before Maj. Branch of the sanitary detachment, working in a blinding, suffocating mask himself, had applied a crude tourniquet.

Nineteen victims of L were headed for Baccarat soon after dawn. The effect of phosgene gas was so treacherous and frequently unsuspected that Pierce did not take any chance, but had bundled all who showed any signs of distress into waiting ambulances.

Hassler had been silent on the stretcher by my side during the ambulance ride, while Stowers above had coughed and muttered incoherent details about the men who had been trapped in the cubbyhole shelters near the company dugout. Pierce, a slim youth of eighteen, had coughed in violent spasms and spit blood on my blankets and blouse. His face had turned a sickening gray-black by the time the stricken collection had been deposited in a receiving ward at Baccarat. Strange people of both sexes, in gowns of rubber, had worked in a frenzy with oxygen tanks before Pierce had coughed his last. The rest of us, separated from Stacy, Hassler, and Swann, had found ourselves in what seemed to be a basement room. Here we had been stripped of all clothing, thoroughly fumigated, and had our heads shaved before we knew what it was all about. I had finally landed in an officers' ward, where most of those, now with me at Vittel, had collected after the first attack. Eyes had been treated, blood-pressure tests made amid rushing nurses and doctors. The bedlam had been accompanied by Preston's coughing spasms and grunting "ugh, ughs." These had finally ceased, behind a screen.

Miss Ross, our nurse, and a visiting chaplain, under our persistent questioning, had reported the deaths of some thirty-odd from the first attacks and of a dozen more out of B, C, and I companies before the day was over. Through similar sources I had learned of the deaths of Hassler and Swann. By some strange prank of hate, Hassler, who was horribly wounded and who never did get a mask on, had outlived his youthful buddy by an hour or so.

It was not until I had gotten my bearings at Vittel, after the spasmodic fears, retches, and pains induced by the powerful suggestion of neighboring hemorrhages, that I had learned about Stacy's death. Marr, of L, had lasted almost two weeks before he, too, had "gone west."

A seemingly simple routine had followed our arrival at Vittel by hospital train—botanic acid in the eyes, no food for several days, liquid diet, and enforced rest for a week or ten days more. Later there had been a little exercise each day, between morning session choking and suffocating in the fumes of camphor steam. My inflamed eyes and a broken membrane in the mouth, evidently caused by zealous efforts to adjust my mouthpiece, had proved little more than temporary inconveniences. These were nothing to the first indescribable fears, when I had coughed, vomited, and wondered if the hemorrhages which had developed among some of those around me in those first hours at Baccarat were to be my fate, too. A cable had gone home as soon as Capt. Marks, the medical officer, had advised, and letters had followed this.

Upon preparing to get out for exercise I found that Stacy's uniform had been substituted for my own, after coming from the fumigator at Baccarat. No doubt some enterprising hospital orderly had decided that the safest way to secure a good "45" was to make a clean sweep of everything. From necessity, therefore, and for reasons of sentiment, I sent the uniform out for slight alterations and to have an officer's band put on the sleeve. I did not know how to reach Stacy's folks and I knew he wouldn't mind.

Thus I evolved within four weeks from a bed case to a walking patient who could look up the stricken L gang in the parks, around the casino, and in the wards of Contrexéville. Stowers, Wallace, Bartram, Parker, Kuhn, Anderson, Brooke, and others seemed to be all right, but Smith, a rather frail lad, would never go back to duty. Perry had a bad infection in the nose from a shell splinter, while David, who had been shot accidentally in Neufmaisons, was pale and wan and suffered the same hell that Barney did.

Rainbow gossip was contributed by those at Vittel and by Turk and Spratling, who came in from Baccarat later. The division had not only left Lorraine for points unknown, but the relief had been accomplished amid heavy shelling and a certain brand of Boche humor. The sausage balloon that usually floated over Cirey could plainly be seen with a huge sign draping its fat side: "Farewell, Forty-second—Welcome Seventy-seventh." This bit of fiction was soon laughed off, but evidence of the Rainbow's departure came in with a group of gassed and wounded from the 77th Division. The Boches had greeted them with a big raid, much as they had introduced themselves to our first battalion in the early days. They had penetrated our old sector almost as far back as Pexonne.

With Barney, Riley, Greer, and others, I attended a ball game between two of the local hospital units, sat out at a dance of nurses, doctors, and a few patients, and hobnobbed in a nearby café with a group of wounded British officers, lately in from the Chemin des Dames.[2] A Cockney in the group, who had been in Flanders, the Dardanelles, and elsewhere, was admittedly feigning exhaustion, a process of faking which we called "goldbricking" and which they called "swinging the lead."

There came a sorrowful day when I wished heartily that I had not forgotten how to cry. Without warning Barney was taken down from his Balkan frame, put in a plaster cast, and shipped to a point on the coast. Surely, I would never have a better buddy or friend than this long-suffering boy of skin and bones, of sad, pained eyes, who was snatched right out of my life, like June had been in a faraway past.

A strange mixture of feelings began to push and pull in the void that Barney left behind. What would Mrs. Mahoney think about me, swingin' the lead when I was fit for duty? What of the third battalion of the 168th Infantry? Where were those men in mustard brown? No matter where they were, there were Tim, Wally, Perce, John, and "Cap" Allen; there was L company, most of whose men I knew well and who knew me; there were the men of the fourth platoon, for nearly all of whom I felt as fierce an attachment as I did for my fellow officers.

A batch of forwarded mail from the regiment brought my desire to follow the Rainbow to fever heat. Old letters from across the Atlantic were devoured, but, after all, June and the homefolks, in fact, everything of the past seemed irrevocably and finally of another planet. The three stale missives in the pack from friends in brown didn't seem stale at all. One was from Perce, who had learned through unnamed sources that I was still above ground and wanted me back. One was from Tim; ditto, only more so. In his letter was a note from Bob

Wickland. Its opening, "Howdy Loot," and messages from the platoon, determined me. Within forty-eight hours I had purchased two duffel bags, secured my discharge and transportation to the concentration center at St. Aignan, said farewell to David and my wardmates, and made a monotonous train journey to the plateau town of Langres, where I had a three-hour stopover between trains. Later I learned that a ten-minute walk in the right direction from Langres' cogwheeled incline station would have taken me to my brother Ben.

St. Aignan, whose main rue seemed a dusty likeness to pictorial conceptions of Stratford-on-Avon, teemed with bustling life. Trucks, camions, native civilians, poilus, doughboys in campaign hats, and snappy officers in barrack caps moved in and out of the dusty thoroughfares like an army of busy bees. It was the Fourth of July, I learned with considerable surprise.

I had supposed that a fellow reported into St. Aignan and right out again for troops. Instead my heart was like lead over the gruff information handed me by the division adjutant. I might never see the Rainbow again. I might be stuck in St. Aignan for the "duration," and I'd be lucky if that were true, according to the natty major who had ordered me to duty with local troops of the 41st Division. He had also advised that I get to looking more like a soldier "toot sweet."

I made my sorrowful way through the crowds, looking for my new command. I saluted passing officers and soldiers in pump-handle fashion until my arm, long out of practice from the laxity of trench and bivouac life, was as heavy as my heart. Was I really to be stuck in this lonely hole? After the agony I had gone through to get my bearings with the Rainbow must I begin all over again with a bunch of strange men?

These distracting thoughts were interrupted by a staff car that rolled by and stopped at the narrow curb. Officers inside were motioning to me. I approached with expectant curiosity, stood at attention, and saluted. The officers chatted with gay nonchalance, while a handsome, gray-haired general "skinned me alive." Didn't I know that trench caps were not according to uniform regulations for the area? Well, I knew it now and the sun must not set upon the unkempt and unmilitary figure

I made. I saluted and marched off, humiliated and more lonely than ever, looking for the road to a neighboring village called Thesée. As I pounded the dust I was aware of the first seeds of suspicion that my life, other than the one I had known in the Rainbow, would never be quite the same again.

Immediate events with my new command caused the seeds to grow into a harvest of bitter truth. A supply sergeant in the dusty town of Thesée fished me out an issue hat, but I was unable to locate an officer's hat cord to go with it. On the way to supper with a group of strange officers and a pompous chaplain, an unknown colonel bawled me out on account of my delinquency in dress. I took it all in at attention, trying to console myself with the thought that I had been rebuked by heaps better men than he.

Homesick, miserable, and physically soft, I sweated profusely in the file closers, as the company hiked out to a field for drill next morning. A session of "squads east and west" in the broiling sun was not so bad, except for a pronounced fatigue. A session of extended-order drill, in command of the third platoon, brought the bitter truth still closer home. The formations and methods of deploying were entirely new to me and, as old Perce would say, "I couldn't turn 'em around in a ten-acre field."

Capt. Sands of K company did his best, I suppose, with a hopeless misfit. He halted the exercises with a brusque "That'll do; that'll do." I went to the sidelines, deeply mortified, as a sergeant took my place. I was glad for the rest period that followed, where men squatted, sprawled, and smoked in the edge of a dusty wood. My new company commander gave a short lecture on gas and gas attacks, emphasizing the idea that the slightest whiff meant death. The conscientious officer, who certainly commanded some splendidly disciplined troops, gave a very realistic word picture of a gas attack, considering the fact that he had never attended one in person. He only omitted a few minor details—men spitting blood on their blankets and turning gray-black; a bloody face on a dugout floor; the mutilated form of a boy whom a fellow loved like his own brother.

I turned in at a lonely, curb-side billet, thoroughly distressed over the knowledge that I would not do. Capt. Sands was quite diplomatic at breakfast. A troop train of four hundred men was heading for the First Division at 8:00 a.m. Capt. Lillard, in command of the train, would need some help. I was to go along with him for the three- or four-day trip and report back to my new command from the unknown point on the front.

Capt. Lillard and a slender looey, with a cordless hat like my own, greeted me on a railway siding. A busy hour was spent loading the train. Raucous, catcalling men bulged from the windows and doors of the tiny, straw-filled cars. The engine panted and heaved, making ready for travel. I was sick at heart and wished I had never left my friends at Vittel. The Rainbow was out of reach forever and I would never see Tim and the bunch again.

An orderly approached briskly, his hobnails mincing along the cinder patch between tracks. He seemed to be in a hurry and to bear important news. He saluted and asked the three of us if we belonged to the 42nd Division. Donahue, the tall looey, and I answered affirmatively in excited unison and immediately became friends. We shared equally in the overwhelming joy caused by a slip of paper, from which the orderly read. The priceless sheet countermanded a series of orders and stated that all officers of the 42nd Division would report to Châlons-sur-Marne, "toot sweet," wherever that enticing place could be. Donahue couldn't contain himself. "Whoopee!" he shouted, as men in the cars looked at him as if he had gone off his head. We left an open-mouthed captain glued in his tracks and scurried off to regimental headquarters for further directions.

Donahue, who had been wounded in the arm early in May, was no more beside himself with happiness than I was. He was just a bit more vociferous. "Boy, I'll follow 'at Rainbow to hell an' gone." As we hiked a dusty road to Noyes to catch a train I gathered that my new buddy's shirt would be in hock to "Wild Bill" Donovan and Father Duffy for quite a spell.[3] He sure had kept the wires "beaucoo hot" with collect telegrams to his regimental friends, hoping to get out of St. Aignan.

We boarded the crowded cars at a rustic station. Two cordless campaign hats went out of the window as the flat wheel of our carriage rattled through Blois and wrinkled trench caps came forth from dusty duffel bags. Donahue and I were now old friends, spiritual union having been almost instantaneous. A physical closeness was necessary in our compartment, which was jammed with French and American officers. The latter talked of new and strange divisions lately landed. I had heard much of the First, Second, and 26th divisions, of course, and knew there was such a thing as a National Army, but the outfits mentioned, numbered in the twenties, thirties, seventies, and eighties, sounded like Greek to me.[4] Donahue, on the other hand, knew all about 'em. Dam' if six or seven of 'em hadn't saluted him while he was condemned to "St. Agony," and his arm hadn't been equal to the occasion.

I munched contentedly on a hunk of French confection as Donahue described the terrible siege of the replacement division with appraising retrospect—"Boy, oh, boy. St. Agony's right—I'll tell th' cockeyed world."[5]

Angry planes droned in the night overhead, when passengers scurried out of the cars at Châlons. Bombs banged into the railway yards and into other parts of the darkness. Crisscrossing beams of light swept the heavens in search of the enemy airmen. Antiaircraft thumped from unseen parts of town. It was the first air raid we had seen and we were more interested with the spectacle than concerned with the results of the descending bombs.

A French poilu in a deserted Red Cross hut directed us to a hotel in one of the pitch-black streets. A shadowy woman with a candelabra led us through a ghostly lobby, down dark, spectral halls to what seemed to be a room. We fell into bed wearily, after removing duffel bags, caps, and shoes. The pounding in town ceased, and we were soon dead to the world.

Early morning brought a skimpy breakfast upon a sun porch, overlooking a plot of weeds, which had once been a garden. The untidy madame announced with gesticulations that folks lived in the cellars in Châlons and only came out with the sun. "Boches, beaucoo boom, boom!" our hostess explained, adding that the Czech lieutenant at an adjoining table was the only other guest.

The streets of Châlons were a riot of color in the July morning sun. Natives pattered along the narrow walks, with shopping baskets on their arms. The dark blue of French officers of high rank dotted the brown of the headquarters square, where we reported for directions to the Rainbow's front. German prisoners policed the dirty gutters. Husky, fine-looking Russians and Chinese coolies repaired twisted tracks in the railway yards. We invaded the Red Cross hut for cigarettes. Inside, a beautiful woman in headdress of white sat beside an ancient cash register, enveloped in a halo of tobacco smoke. Lithe, black Senegalese in bloomers, and fez-like caps, many of them with withered Boche ears hung on strings around their necks, shuffled in and out. Moroccans in turbans and pantaloons, poilus in dusty horizon blue, and a scattering of doughboys came and went among the smelly tables, all paying homage to the beautiful lady, which seemed to indicate that she was not of this world.

We hit a road for the front, Donahue indulging in a lot of unintelligible chatter about Dillons, Monahans, O'Hagans, and a fellow named Kilmer in his outfit who wrote poetry or something.[6] Artillery thumped in the distance and the road was camouflaged in spots. A crib-like wagon loaded with old men and women and sundry belongings left an unknown village. Artillery caissons, trucks, motorcycles, rumbling and spluttering north and south, covered us with a chalk-like dust. We hiked several sweaty kilometers and thumbed a ride on a truck for a few more. The Irish from New York were about ten kilometers ahead, in a wood beyond a place called Jonchery-sur-Suippes, while the Iowa crowd was "somewheres off to the right on th' fer side of a place called just plain Suippes." The Rainbow was with the Frogs and "big doin's was comin', toot sweet."

The truck prepared to turn off. Donahue and I separated regretfully in the battered town of St. Hilaire. After several perspiring kilometers more a supply wagon headed for the

151st Machine-Gun Battalion picked me up. I knew I was nearing friends now and could hardly wait. I finally descended in a clump of woods, where a cluster of dusty barracks was surrounded by shelters carved into the hard, white chalk.

Men snored in pup tents around my camouflaged cradle of boards, nailed from tree to tree. Other men snored in nearby pup tents and in bunks like my own. I was weary, but could not sleep for the belching guns in the dark woods behind.

A series of lately received impressions passed in review. Col. Lennert, Col. Townes, Maj. Bronson, and Capt. Norton had quizzed me about my immediate past in their underground shelter, calling me Tommy, as though there were no difference between ages and rank. The major had taken me outside, pointed into a dusty thicket, and bade me get up there where I belonged. I had hiked forward with eager hobnails, passing half-hidden guns, crossing a narrow-gauged railway, passing more guns, wagons, water carts, rolling kitchens, and men in brown and blue, through a picket line of horses, across trenches cut into the chalk, around a shack and by a rolling kitchen. Finally, I had been confronted with exclamations from shirtless cooks and with a familiar baritone, "Well, I'm a son of a sea cook; look who's here." Men, sitting in the woods, tailor-fashion, had left off "reading shirts" to welcome me and to ply me with questions about their missing friends. Others had scrambled out of pup tents in stocking feet and exposed shirttails to crowd around. George Knabe and the once despised Jim Bonner, who had been transferred to L during my absence, had added their share of back-whacking greetings. Wally had said less than the others, as usual, but had poked me in the ribs significantly and had grinned like a Cheshire cat at mess. The K crowd had been located in a nearby shelter, where Tim finally recovered sufficiently to give me the latest news from an important spot in the Cumberland Mountains. John had ceased shaving a fuzzy chin to give me a shake. He had attacked a dusty blouse with a vigorous brush before the L family departed and the enormous "Cap" Allen had chuckled over John's only vice—"That guy'd try to keep clean in a coal mine."

A big railroad gun in the woods left a twinge of discomfort in the temples and ears with each muffled thump that echoed through the night. Someone said that we were in the Champagne, but just what part of France the undefined section was a rather hazy affair. Big doings were coming soon. "Well, what of it, what of it?" I mused, tossing in my bunk, wide-eyed, but thoroughly contented. By golly I was home.

Village Negre, 168th Infantry, Badonviller, April 24, 1918. Courtesy U.S. Army Signal Corps.

Funeral, 1st Battalion, 168th Infantry, June 7, 1918. Courtesy U.S. Army Signal Corps.

Chapel, 168th Infantry, June 7, 1918. Courtesy U.S. Army Signal Corps.

Camp, 168th Infantry and 151st Field Artillery Regiment, near Suippes, June 8, 1918. Courtesy U.S. Army Signal Corps.

Gen. John J. Pershing and General Menoher, Châtel, June 28, 1918.
Courtesy U.S. Army Signal Corps.

Maj. S. H. Humbough, 42nd Division staff, paying his last respects to 2nd Lt. R. E. Creaton, Company H, 168th Infantry, near Pexonne, August 6, 1918. Courtesy U.S. Army Signal Corps.

Machine gunner, Seicheprey, St. Mihiel, September 12, 1918. Courtesy National Archives.

Company B, 165th Infantry, near Hazavant, St. Mihiel, September 14, 1918.
Courtesy National Archives.

Lieutenant Hugh S.
Thompson, 1919.
Courtesy Hugh S.
Thompson, M.D.

Hugh S. Thompson. Courtesy Hugh S. Thompson, M.D.

CHAPTER TWELVE

Wounded Again

orty-eight hours in the hot and dusty thickets of the Champagne afforded a working knowledge of what the labyrinth of trenches, the dugouts, the barricades, the camouflage, and the thumping artillery were all about. Perce and Wally explained the defensive setup for the big doings to come, while Sergt. Ford was outfitting me with mask, helmet, web belt, and "45."

A walk with Beavers, Jensen, and three or four others to the northern edge of the woods was even more enlightening. A flat expanse ahead was divided by a snake-like road of white, whose mouth was joined by trenches on either side and guarded by movable barricades of metal and wire. The desolate plain was crisscrossed by gray-white parapets and dotted here and there with patches of stubble and scrub pines. Myriad poppies, blood red against the chalk, danced in the shimmering waves of July heat. Out there a couple of kilometers or so two regiments of French held the first line of our front. A kilometer behind them was a second line of unseen poilus, New Yorkers, Ohioans, Alabamans, and Iowa troops of our own second battalion. The advance troops were to fall back to this second line in case the expected assault should come on full force.[1]

Back in the woods the trenches of K, L, and M, supported by I, which ran through our bivouac of pup tents, tree cradles, and rustic barracks, constituted a reserve for the present and a secondary defense should withdrawal of the forward line become necessary.

I lost no time getting acquainted with the new men of the fourth platoon, in helping McDonough select four stretcher-bearers, and in identifying the L company trenches. These were joined on the left by K and M, with more Alabamans beyond them. Our first battalion abutted our right and was in turn joined by the Alpine Chasseurs of the French 46th Division. A company of Georgia and Pennsylvania machine gunners and our own machine-gun company were parts of the immediate scheme. A reserve company of machine gunners, the South Carolina and California engineers, our "one-pounders," the Maryland mortars, were in our rear. Artillery of various calibers, both French and American, was hidden in the brush with camouflage behind the battalion headquarters shack and the adjoining sanitary detachment.

An order from Gen. Gouraud, the commander of the Fourth French Army, which had been read to troops shortly before my return and which was now paraphrased for me by all and sundry, seemed to reduce our job to simple, if awe-inspiring, terms. No matter what happened, the Fourth French Army and its integral part, the Rainbow, were to remain in their tracks. "The bombardment will be terrible," Wally quoted from memory. ". . . None shall glance to the rear; none shall yield a step. Each shall have but one thought, to kill, to kill many until the Boches have had enough . . . ."

Battalion officers' meetings offered snatch visits and reunions with Melvin, Turk, and the rest of the K bunch, with Cullen and Van of M, with Capt. Moore, High, and Albert of I, and with Dorsey, who had been transferred to M when George Knabe and Jim Bonner had been sent to L. So the cocky Jim had been granted his wish to get out of the supply company and into a line outfit.

A map in Maj. Bronson's possession gave a rough picture of the Fourth Army's whole front. We seemed to be in the center of a thirty-five- or forty-kilometer stretch, extending from Rheims on the left to the edge of a wooded area marked "Argonne Forest" on the right. A letter went to my Dad, hint-

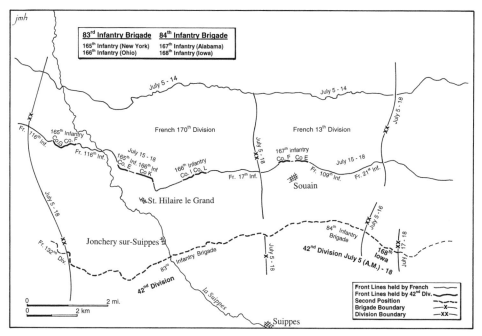

jmh

83rd Infantry Brigade	84th Infantry Brigade
165th Infantry (New York)	167th Infantry (Alabama)
166th Infantry (Ohio)	168th Infantry (Iowa)

July 5 - 14

July 5 - 14

July 5 - 18

French 170th Division

French 13th Division

Fr. 116th Inf.

165th Infantry
Co. G Co. F

Fr. 116th Inf.

July 15 - 18

165th Inf. 166th Inf.
Co. E   Co K

166th Infantry
Co. I Co. L

167th infantry
Co. F Co E

July 15 - 18

Fr. 17th Inf.

Fr. 109th Inf.

Fr. 21st Inf.

Souain

July 5 - 18

St. Hilaire le Grand

July 5 - 18

July 5 - 16

84th Infantry
Brigade

Fr. 132nd Div.

Jonchery sur-Suippes

42nd Division July 5 (A.M.) - 18

168th
Iowa

July 17 - 18

July 5 - 18

83rd Infantry Brigade

42nd Division

la Suippes

0 _____ 2 mi.
0 _____ 2 km

Front Lines held by French	
Front Lines held by 42nd Div.	
Second Position	
Brigade Boundary	—x—
Division Boundary	—xx—

Suippes

Champagne-Souain area. Map by John M. Hollingsworth.

ing at our general location. We were about fifteen miles in front of a certain well-known river, while the city of the famous cathedral was about as far to our left as Ringgold is from Chattanooga.

A walk with Wally, George, Albert, and High to a place called Souain on the map disclosed a huge mine crater, an expanse of debris and flattened buildings, in the midst of which stood the side walls of what had once been a church. Frenchmen and a regiment of American Negro troops held that neck of the woods. Doughboys, naked to the waist, "read shirts" in the brush between. A stocking-footed group played "one-eyed cat" with an indoor baseball in a pine-bordered clearing along the route. Gaunt horses munched fodder under the scrubby trees and in picket lines, camouflaged by transplanted saplings. The woods seemed filled with brown and blue ants, wagons, pup tents, rustic huts, and belching, half-hidden guns.

We stumbled upon the skeleton of a French poilu, half-buried in the chalky dust. The uniform was decaying, the shoes weather-beaten and tattered, the dented helmet caked with rust. We examined the gruesome souvenir of bleached bones with the aid of hobnail toes and wondered how burying details had missed a fellow who must have lain after some past battle in plain view.

False alarms of the coming attack began to develop by night, bringing us out of our bivouac above ground and into the surrounding trench position. In the midst of my platoon I felt somewhat doubtful about the immediate future, but was without regrets over being at home. The drumfire of friendly artillery and livid star shells and rockets splotched the dark skies ahead.

Between alerts, which were like so many fire drills, I picked up the gossip of the last days in Lorraine; of the recent surprise visit Wally had had from his uncle, who had come to France with the "Y"; of John's promotion and Cherub's boost in rank and transfer to the second battalion; of the punishing hikes that had brought the Rainbow from Meurthe to the Champagne. Twilight visits with the K, M, and I crowds were sources of real comradeship. A cable from the Mahoneys to Perce, received a few days before my return, was a fount of satisfaction and thrills. "Do everything possible, Lieut. Thompson, our expense," read the message from Harold's faraway folks, who had evidently seen my name in the casualty lists of Iowa papers. I was even more touched when Wolf, Getty, Stack, and other stocking-footed, half-naked cootie hunters, once of Sioux City, explained that the Mahoneys had little money to be chucking away.

Latrine gossip had a new time for the big event each day. "Grapevine telegraph," seeping into the late twilights of the dusty brush, where we hobnobbed with French artillerymen from nearby guns, now set the date for the attack at midnight of the thirteenth–fourteenth. The hours passed, but the Boches remained ominously quiet, despite the activity of our guns. Electrifying news came down on the morning of the fourteenth. French units, with a company of Rainbow troops, had raided the enemy lines ahead early in the night and had come back with a rich haul of prisoners. Third-degree methods had brought precise information and the first-line troops had been immediately ordered to retire to the secondary positions. Runners bore the news that the Boche artillery would go into action at ten minutes after midnight on the morrow. The hordes of enemy infantry would jump off behind a creeping barrage at 4:15 A.M.

I skipped over to see Tim in the late afternoon. "I'll be seeing you, toot sweet," he assured in parting, as John and the others came to the door. There was a friendly scuffle and some banter as I left and Tim's galloping laugh followed me through the woods. Passing the big dugout in rear of our trenches, the barrack that housed part of my platoon and the cluster of pup tents that sheltered the rest, I was back with the L family again. Tins of slum were consumed around a smoking kitchen on wheels. A round was made to see that the men were sticking close to their side arms and guns and to be sure that they understood what they were to do. Orders had said that we were to man the trenches at the first signs of Boche artillery.

A twilight gabfest followed with the gesticulating Frenchmen, who finally left for their guns. We strolled back to our tree cradles, Perce indulging in expletives about the queer Frogs. They were always overrating the "krautheads" and then knockin' hell out of 'em every time they got fresh. We were still busy at nervous small talk when every gun in the Allied armies broke loose in a flashing, vomiting roar.

My heart began to pound a bit, but there was a peculiar sense of comfort in Stacy's blouse, which had been with me ever since Vittel. McDonough and Owen appeared by my side in the din and my growing case of fidgets was calmed, somewhat.

A whizzing shell banged behind the invisible orderly room shack. A brace of "77's" bang, banged with livid flashes farther in the woods. A covey of "88's" screamed off to our left, followed by nervous bursts of musketry from somewhere. We started for the trenches and had made but a few yards when the woods became a torrent of whizzing, roaring, flashing, deafening hell.

We groped forward through the roaring, flashing thunder. Men stumbled over each other in the trench bottoms. The darkness was now violet and now splotched with green, yellow, and red flames of fire. Gravel rained upon our helmets, trees fell, we choked in swirls of dust. We tripped over a figure, whose piercing screams sounded muffled in the terrifying din. Now shadowy, now vivid forms huddled against the walls of the fire trench. A frenzied, yelling checkup revealed that some fifteen men were missing. McDonough was left in charge of the trench while Lawson, Owen, and I made for the pup tents of the fourth platoon. Flashing detonations filled the woods, the whine of shells half-obscured by the thundering noise. We staggered through stretches of trench and crawled around a series of erupting bayous. Stretcher-bearers stumbled by in the choking dust, their yelling, "Gangway, gangway," soft under the blanket of fearful, volcanic sound.

We crawled out on top of the ground near the orderly room shack and groped, cringing through a shower of rocks. We became entangled in tent ropes and equipment. Livid flashes revealed a peculiar, kaleidoscopic view of men crawling toward us on all fours. There was a blinding, deafening flash. Lurid, shuttle-like glimpses into the raging darkness now gave a ghastly picture of bodies sprawled in a mass of gore. We squirmed about among the pup tents yelling familiar names and finally gave it up.

Running pell-mell above ground, crawling in and out of hellish trenches, we reached the platoon barracks; a distraught mule galloped past and fell into a trench back of us as we ran frantically through the barrack door and into flickering candlelight. Blinding flashes, roaring guns, even deep-seated fear evaporated momentarily at the fantastic sight within. I stopped dead in my tracks. My brain, as if dulled by strong drink, refused to take it all in. A group of new men huddled in a haze of candlelight and dust. A dead man, with distorted, unrecognizable features lay on his back, an expanse of crimson around his face and neck. Dust poured through jagged holes in the barrack wall in a suction-like stream. Bunce hung over a sawhorse of drying undershirts. How queer, how queer that Bunce should be looking for something in the chalky barrack floor at a time like this. No, he was trying to reach the dead man's gun, that's what it was. Seconds were ages as Owen and I stood transfixed. The peculiar noise outside kept up. I became aware that blood dripped from my sergeant's limp, outstretched hand. The roaring outside came back, full force. Woolly senses were gathered with great effort. "We've got to get Bunce into a trench." The fantastic scene had become real now and we worked fast. I grabbed the unconscious figure by the collar and Owen took his legs. We struggled through the door as Lawson prodded the other men in the hazy candlelight. There was a blinding flash and a dull thud near the end of the barrack. I heard the faint sound of crashing timber as I fell.

I picked myself up to find that Bunce and the others had been swallowed up in the roaring night. My left arm pained like fury and something warm and gooey was running down my sleeve. "I've got to get to the platoon position, somehow," I muttered in a half daze. My back throbbed under a shoulder blade and my right side burned like fire. I groped around in the thundering darkness as if in a bad dream. A green flare cast a sickening pallor into the roaring, belching yellows and reds. "Jesus, it's gas!" I scrambled into a trench, trying to manage my mask with one hand. Somebody knocked my helmet off. Strange hands worked roughly around my face and I found myself on my feet. Arms were around my waist. Half-stumbling, half-falling, I staggered blindly along with those who helped me, as if in a trance. What were these people trying to do to me? What was all the crazy noise about? Oh, yes, I had been wounded, that's what it was. The throbbing pain and a sense of sticky breeches came back.

My mask was off now and I was vaguely conscious that the gas alarm was false. Shadowy figures appeared and disappeared in the flashing clouds of dust, faces gray and bayonets flickering in the roaring lights. Owen was by me, that's who it was—and McDonough, too. How wonderful to feel these friends of flesh and blood. Measureless time passed in the flashing, roaring, choking night. My brain reeled with a crazy exhilaration and I was conscious of an overpowering weakness. My arm ached. Other parts of my body burned like fury, but how delicious was the muddled knowledge that others would have to carry on. Dead men were out under the falling trees, I knew, although my thoughts raced in an insane stream. Where was poor Bunce? How about Tim and Wally and all the rest? The answers to these half-dozen questions were drowned in the hot sweat of my body, which was now turning to ice. A ball of cotton seemed to be stuffed into my throat. An ear-splitting flash of lightning seared the shadowy branches overhead with an electrifying, ghastly crash. There was a shower of tree limbs and rocks. A scream beyond me in the trench penetrated my giddy thoughts. For the first time in my twenty-three years I passed out.

I came to choking in clouds of dust and blinking in a haze of candlelight. Someone was sticking a sponge in my mouth. A strange pounding overhead caused flakes of chalk to crumble from shaking timbers above, covering me with white grit. Confused wits gathered themselves again and I was conscious of pain. I knew those around me now, except the gray-faced, bloody ones who sprawled in all sorts of positions in the dust. That was Maj. Branch with the sponge. And the dim, dust-covered figure who barked muffled orders to Ery and a group of men as they clambered up the dugout stairs was Maj. Bronson.

The confused scene was enveloped in darkness as the candles flickered out. Wounded men yelled above the pounding above, "Jesus, gimme air! Water! Water!" A panic seemed to be taking place under the blanket of thumping, suffocating darkness. Somebody was trying to get the candles going again. Muffled orders. Scraping feet. Groaning wounded. Lights once more. Feet shuffled on the dugout stairs. Men were circling 'round and 'round, climbing one set of stairs and stumbling down another. Drafts of powder-tainted air blew the candle flames about, but an excruciating thirst was somewhat relieved.

Grunting, struggling stretcher-bearers, covered with dust, dumped wounded on the dugout floor. Crimson and dust.

Crimson and dust. I recognized one of the ashen faces near me. It was Davis of my platoon. Blood had soaked through the front of his blouse. He lay with eyes closed, very still.

Lieut. Green of the sanitary detachment working over the wounded finally rolled me over in the dust. He grasped my bad hand and I winced. He removed my pistol belt, pulled my blouse back roughly, tore my undershirt to shreds and slit my right breeches leg with an unseen instrument. I was fully conscious now, but lay still in an overpowering, languorous helplessness. My arm was bound to my blouse with a crude sling. The figure who knelt over me was telling Maj. Brewer about my wounds. He couldn't see the arm, but thought it was broken. There was a paralysis of the hand. A shell fragment had torn a tunnel under my shoulder blade and there was a long knife-like slash in the soft flesh over the kidney and hip. He couldn't tell whether I was injured internally or not, but I had bled a lot and seemed to be badly shocked. I tried to move to test out the medical officer's alarming doubts. I was sore all over and sank back in a numbed stillness again, mind racing with thoughts of internal injuries.

Maj. Bronson's worried face and muffled voice brought instincts of self-preservation to the fore. I heard every ominous word that he said. It was three o'clock. The Boches would be starting at four and he didn't want any of the wounded trapped below ground. Muffled, shouted orders now obscured the pounding above. Gray-faced, crimson-jacketed men coughed, opened dilated eyes, and seemed to sleep again under the shaking timbers and crumbling chalk. Stretcher-bearers worked in a new frenzy now, clearing the floor of wounded men. I felt a wild desire to be above ground and demanded that Lieut. Green get me into my pistol belt again. I had about decided to climb the stairs the best way I could when two men lifted me on a stretcher and made for the shadowy door. The litter was steep and I held on with my good hand to keep from falling off. The men sweated to the top of the roaring stairs. A draught of air was delicious, but was forgotten at the first blinding flash. I was sorry I had not remained where I was. The stretcher-bearers struggled through the savage maelstrom.

My wounds were forgotten for raw fear. "God, was this to keep up forever?" A flaming thud snatched the thought from my brain. I hit the trench bottom on my head and shoulders. The man on the rear end of the litter was hit and the other man crawled over me to his aid. Stretcher-bearers, carrying heavy loads through the nerve-shattering din, stumbled over me in the trench. I crawled desperately through the flying grit trying to get back to the dugout, but the shadowy traffic prevented. I turned about painfully and groped after the procession that was becoming visible in the fantastic, livid, thundering dawn.

I lay on my side in an unknown strip of trench. Ery, who had appeared from nowhere, lay by me, his head bare and black hair matted with blood. A spray of rockets lighted the violet dawn. The livid flashes, the roaring dust, hadn't let up since midnight, which now seemed a week past. A fellow had once been a man, but now he was a cowering, cringing worm.

Ery and I crawled and hobbled after the silent line of stretchers around bayou after bayou. We finally made a wide, shallow trench, congested with gory, dust-covered traffic. Screaming shells came on trenchwise and erupted near the I company positions. Sheer necessity was teaching me that I could get about handily enough. We crawled through the mass of prone men and neared a shelter of corrugated iron, where men with Red Cross brassards on their arms worked feverishly with bandages, tourniquets, and injections of opiates. Deathly fear did not keep me from marveling at their courage. Frenchmen lay among the dusty figures in brown. Flesh was crimson, arms and legs were soaked in drying blood. A ghastly figure with eyes closed had lost his legs below the knees. Strips of dirty under drawers were tied tightly above the awful stumps. A fellow couldn't recognize his best friend among the gray-faced men. Some bandaged faces and crimson breasts gave no sign of either life or death. A few showed no signs of blood at all.

I tried a thousand ways to keep my mind off the monotonous, crashing shells. Each one that screamed softly above the din seemed destined for me and me alone. A projectile crashed at the head of the trench. A Frenchman and a litter disappeared. The thumping roar became mixed with an almost imperceptible drone overhead. A flock of yellow-bellied planes circled and banked above, their black crosses showing plainly. They swooped low over a clearing in our rear. All but the frightfully wounded ate the dust. The trench was filled with flying lead. The Boche ships swarmed in the barrage, repeating their machine-gun assaults on the trenches several times. "Crazy people," I thought. "You could scour the lunatic asylums and find no one who'd fly in that rain of shells."

The incessant roar seemed human in its anger. I had lost all sense of time in the churning, thundering fire, but it was full day.

Dearing, of L, hobbled through the wounded with an arm in a sling. The bombardment lulled a bit, as if some huge hand had throttled down myriad humming turbines. The woods were being strafed with intermittent high explosive and shrapnel, the whining of shells becoming more pronounced as the barrage lulled, grew, and dwindled again. Stretcher-bearers brought news that the Boche had been stopped cold on the second line. Wounded men took the word as though it made no difference.[2]

Distant musketry mingled with the strafing shells that now banged behind me. Men began to talk and smoke. A procession of stretchers moved to the end of the trench, where burdens were lifted onto the open ground. Several dead were removed from litters to make room for those who still lived. Ery and I were offered a ride, but refused. The fiendish shelling might now be over and a fellow felt that he could manage himself with more safety, free and standing up.

Walking wounded hobbled by the side of the gray-faced burdens under a heavy haze of dust. The line buckled and halted in the midday sun and wound like a snake into the edge of a clearing. Ambulances were collecting just off a distant road. The battalion headquarters shack and an adjoining barracks were masses of debris and splintered timbers. A group of dead lay sprawled among the scattered tents of the I company positions. Trees were broken and prone. The line squirmed and hobbled by a demolished rolling kitchen. Equipment and blankets were strewn about. The pounding had ceased in the woods now, but there was an intermittent fire beyond the road.

The line of dust and crimson moved forward after a short halt. A water cart to the right was overturned and a half-naked figure in brown lay near a broken wheel. A long picket line of dusty horses lay dead. Several quivering beasts wandered aimlessly about and a single animal whinnied pitifully with a ghastly wound in its flank. Grimy figures, naked to the waist, smoked in a clump of brush near a "75" and another gun which was mangled and overturned.

Men were silent as the ambulances received their crimson loads and struggled up a bank to the road, motors groaning and wheels spinning in dust. A few gray-faced figures demanded water and smokes from those who were still on their feet.

Ery and I lay down to wait for the traffic of frightfully wounded to clear up. A man from the sanitary detachment examined the bedraggled looey's head and ordered him into an ambulance. A huge covey of Boche planes swarmed overhead and scattered over the woods, their red bellies blood-like in the bright sun. I breathed a sigh of nervous shaking relief as they disappeared and examined my physical self. My mouth was full of grit, my good hand was bloody, and from the looks of a torn breeches leg, which hung down over my wrap legging, I had bled like a stuck pig. I was conscious again of a painful throb in my wounded arm, which I had bumped against the trench in a scramble from the droning, chattering planes. My other wounds burned like fury once more.

Dearing and I finally got in an ambulance with two badly wounded men. One was bandaged about the head. A pasty mixture of dust and blood smeared his mouth and chin. The other screamed with a shattered hip when the ambulance bumped up the bank. He screamed again as the driver throttled down and changed gears. The latter yelled through the cubbyhole above my head that shells were hitting near the road. The droning motor drowned out most of the whizzing of stray shells, but raw, quivering nerves lent the illusion that one was still in the terrifying fantastic roar. I wondered vaguely how Tim, John, and all the others had fared in the awful mess. The answer to these confused questions seemed nothing like as important as the fact that I was out of the volcano with my life.

The ambulance lunged at a whizzing shell. The wounded man cried with pain. The vehicle began to roll slowly at an even rate of speed and the driver called through the cubbyhole, "It's okay now, buddy, I ain't gonna jerk you no more."

CHAPTER THIRTEEN

Recovery

The ambulance in which Dearing, the two I company men, and I were riding rumbled through a cluster of buildings, hummed along an endless ribbon of dust, and lunged into a stretch of pavement. Carson groaned with his fractured hip when the vehicle came to a jerky halt in Châlons. We were lowered into the gutter of a narrow street. Mabry, whose bandaged head lay at my feet, asked Dearing for a cigarette and light. Throbbing body and quivering nerves could not smother a muddled exultation over being out of the Champagne alive.

A fleet of incoming ambulances added to the pile of dusty, blood-stained wounded near the curb. French stretcher-bearers lugged heavy loads up a ramp, which led into a building of somber stone. The sound of ominous thunder was wafted from somewhere on the distant front. Shells of large caliber pounded off and on in nearby parts of town.

Loud conversation, developing between ambulance drivers and a gesticulating interpreter, seemed to indicate that we were in the wrong place. The hospital was already overflowing with wounded, we heard with dismay. Doughboys had been crammed in with poilus, despite the Frenchmen's understanding that an American hospital had been set up somewhere in the neighborhood for the Rainbow's casualties.

A figure in horizon blue went among the stretchers, baring arms and injecting antitetanus with a rapier-like needle.

Carson's pain was eased by opiates from French hands. The same hands propped his broken limb upon a wad of hairy blankets.

Long-range artillery still banged in town when an American Red Cross man appeared from nowhere and proceeded to straighten out the mess of misunderstanding. He was soon assuring us that we would be taken care of in the hospital as rapidly as bed space was made available by the dying. Meanwhile our benefactor knelt over the battered men, taking cable messages home. Coming to Mabry, he discovered that our ambulance mate had passed away. Mabry dead? It couldn't be. Why, he had demanded a smoke only a few minutes ago. How unreal it all seemed. A few hours before the Champagne had pulsated with brown and blue life. And now, men lay mangled and dead for miles around. Yesterday a fellow was bound to old friends by hoops of steel. Today they were all but forgotten for new friends of fleeting time. Could it be true that Mabry had told me his name, talked of Creston, Iowa, through blood-smeared lips, called me "Loot," as if he had known me always, and flickered out, all in a brief hour or so?

Feet scraped along the curb by my head and Dearing disappeared, amid the grunts of sweaty Frenchmen. "Bien des blesses, bien des blesses," grimaced the talkative stretcher-bearers, as though a man couldn't see that there were many wounded, with his own eyes. I was separated from Carson while we were being toted along the ramp, up a winding stairway and through halls filled with loaded stretchers. Muffled groans mingled with shuffling feet and a variety of metallic sounds. Nurses in white bustled about in the ward to which I was carried.

I was finally shorn of Stacy's blouse by an orderly, while a group of wounded poilus and an unknown doughboy looked on from a row of cots. A nurse, with a Croix de Guerre upon her bosom, stripped me of shoes, leggings, and bloody, ragged pants. I winced as the wounded arm was handled with rough haste by a demon in blood-splattered robe. A shell fragment the size of a bullet had pierced the limb midway between the elbow and wrist. Turned on my stomach by my tormentor, I bit into the blankets when he squeezed the flesh around my body wounds, evidently trying to learn whether they were free of metal. Sopping bandages were applied. I recovered the highly prized blouse from the vanishing attendant. Medical officer and nurses vanished, talking and gesticulating, after getting me into a bed jacket. The Frenchman next to me offered wine from a basket under his cot. He had been shot in the leg in April. Details of the mishap followed, with waving arms, musical sounds, and a series of knuckle raps on his plaster cast.

Our side of the ward was filled with men suffering from a variety of gunshot wounds. I wondered about the empty beds opposite. The vacancy was explained when a group of white-robed, blood-stained men and women stumbled in, mumbling irritably, and fell upon the bunks. The snores of this exhausted operating room crew soon rasped above the hospital noises and the occasional shell explosions outside.

Panting Frenchmen deposited a blood-soaked chasseur near the foot of my cot. I gazed at the grimy figure in rusty blue, the young gray face, eyebrows and tousled hair powdered with chalk dust. A matronly nurse began to remove the unconscious man's clothes. She blanched with fear at the sight of wicked-looking grenades found in the pockets of the disheveled blouse. She carried the bombs into the hall, one at a time, as if each was a live snake, and returned to take up her sanguinary job. She stopped abruptly before the still figure. "Il est mort." she exclaimed, feeling hurriedly for a dusty pulse. I gazed at the dead man's set, ashen face, as the nurse called to attendants for help. I gazed some more, while she pattered about, tear-eyed, among the wounded, muttering to herself, "C'est triste. C'est dommage. Si jeune, si jeune."[1]

A dim light shone in the noisy, ether-laden hall. Blankets screened the windows of the sultry room. Another operating crew shuffled in, waked the snorers opposite, and fell into the beds made vacant by those just aroused. A noticeable bustle seemed to grow above the din of hospital sounds and labored breathing. Shadowy nurses huddled against the walls, nervous half-whispers mingling with a diabolical buzz.

"Boches, ici."

"Avions, avions."

"Beaucoo boom, boom."

The night outside was filled with angry drones. Antiaircraft thumped away at the whining planes. Muffled detonations split the night. I held my breath as two deafening bombs struck close. God, what if one of those things should crash through the roof? I tried to control this new type of fear with thoughts of the sprawling figures on the beds across the way. Why, those women actually slept.

The buzzing planes, the pounding outside kept up, increasing the nameless, helpless dread. For hours, the marauders circled overhead, it seemed.

Tired body ached for rest and sleep, but raw, threadbare nerves would not permit. The whining finally died away. Breathing came easier as scraping feet and suppressed excitement were born again in the hall. I lay wide-eyed in the fetid, gasping night.

More wounded came into the ward soon after breakfast, causing the snoring operating force to move out to make room for them. I wondered when the doctors would get to me as the long day wore on. My French comrade presented me with a snapshot of himself and tried to pacify my growing anxiety, "Bien des blesses, bien des blesses." There seemed nothing to do but lay still, waiting expectantly, with my burning wounds. Wait I did, through the sultry afternoon and through another interminable night of angry planes, exploding bombs, and panic-stricken groans. I was a wreck the next morning, when a pair of Frenchmen lifted me upon an operating cart. Gray-faced traffic was heavy in the hall and in a ward of crimson bandages and Balkan frames, as I rolled through. Shortly, I was in a veritable butcher shop, where several gory operations were going on. The place reeked with ether and the smell of human flesh. The white-robed workers, laboring over anaesthetized victims, were splattered with blood. A trickling stream emptying into a floor drain was colored with crimson dye.

I was thrown summarily upon my belly. Rough hands swabbed my shoulder and side with liquid fire. I bit my lips.

These Frenchmen must not hear me scream. Somebody was holding me in a sitting position now, while unseen hands swathed my body with sheaths of bandage. I felt giddy as an attendant grabbed the tender arm. A menacing figure approached, his forceps dangling with dripping gauze. I shut my eyes in an icy sweat. A red-hot instrument pierced the punctured arm. I grunted in agonized helplessness, squirmed violently to be free from the fiends. The terrorizing instrument was withdrawn from the wound. The savage doctor sawed the gauze back and forth through the throbbing, pulsating hole—"Please, please—!" For the second time in my life I fainted dead away.

The Frenchman in the next cot gave me wine when I came to on my smelly bunk. The matronly nurse wiped my brow. I quivered all over from the shock of unexpected torture. I gathered during the lengthening day that there was neither time, opiates, nor anaesthetic to be spared for any but the desperately hurt.

The angry buzzing marauders came again that night. Nerve-racking explosions banged in the outer darkness. God, was a man never to get any rest?

The air was good outside the following morning, when I was loaded into an ambulance with the doughboy from the ward and two other wounded mates. The driver assured us that the Boche bombers had not located the American hospital, for which we were headed. It was about ten kilometers beyond Châlons. Nerves soothed by this comfort information, I fell into a fitful dream.

The hot sun baking through the canvas of the hospital tent cast a sepia glow over the rows of cots and their bandaged inhabitants. I had caught a glimpse of ripe wheat, a railway siding, a flagpole, and sundry tent walls as stretcher-bearers had lugged me into the foul, humid air of the tarpaulin ward. We were in a place called Ecury, according to Delacorte of the 165th in the next bunk. I was soon dead to the world.

A nurse with a food tray woke me from a heavy sleep. I ate a snack and took stock of my physical self. The same swathing bandages that bound my heavily splinted arm to my side were wrapped around my body in such profusion that I could hardly move. Wounded companions from the New York, Ohio, and Alabama regiments introducing themselves from nearby cots, heard my story of bomb-filled nights and assured me that we were safe from the Boche planes. I became unconscious with sleep again.

Excited voices jerked me from a fantastic dream into a strange blanket of darkness. Where was I? Confused senses returned. Thumping bombs and antiaircraft in the distance were partially smothered by the buzzing of myriad planes. Nurses, doctors, and walking patients seemed to be shuffling outside to watch the searchlights over Châlons. I thanked my lucky stars that I was free from the marauders at last. A series of shouts from the night chased these thoughts out of my head. "Boches. Boches. They're comin' this way!" Doctors, nurses, patients, all who could possibly move, scrambled out of the tents and into the fields. An angry drone grew above the distant buzzing and became a maddening roar.

The shadowy bird swooped above the patch of chalk dust and wheat, in which we lay trembling. The plane, flying low, circled the area, headed south, and started back toward the tents. There was a deafening explosion near the flagpole. Panic-stricken screams came from under the canvas. The airman circled again. A chattering, flashing machine gun poured lead into the canvas walls. The lone bomber buzzed off in the night. The blackness was alive with pandemonium. Cries came from a stricken tent. Wounded victims had been struck. We lay still in the wheat, expecting the winged devil to come back. Another plane, wings red and green with signal lights, droned in the darkness to bring another siege of dread. The sultry night was filled with an audible, mass sigh when the ship was found to be an Allied plane. Crowds hobbled back to the tents. The friendly plane continued to patrol the area, even though the momentarily forgotten searchlights and noises over Châlons had ceased. It was morning before the panic died down.

An investigation by day disclosed that the bomb had fallen in the open space around the flagpole, scattering two lines of gravel and slag, which had been poured in the form of a cross to mark the world of canvas as a hospital. The bomber had flown so low that it seemed impossible that his missile of death had failed to hit among the tents. There seemed to be nothing that could have prevented him from wrecking the place. Everyone was convinced that, despite probable orders from the enemy High Command, a spark of individual humanity had kept the Boche airman from doing more damage than he did.

Day brought further acquaintance with my ward mates and a surprise visit from a former L company man. Renault had been transferred to division headquarters in the early days, owing to his ability to speak French. He was now engaged in locating and sorting the Rainbow's wounded, who lay scattered about in surrounding hospitals. From him I got piecemeal information of my regiment's fate in the volcanic Champagne. He had seen troops of the 168th in town a few nights before. They had been relieved in the lines and were headed for God knows where. The Boches had been badly butchered and stopped cold all along the Fourth French Army's front. We had lost as many men killed and over half as many wounded in the twelve-hour bombardment as we had lost during our whole stay in the trenches of Lorraine. Lieuts. Little, Ery, Dorsey, and Cullen were lying wounded in hospitals a few kilometers away. Lieuts. Gerry and Hunt of the second battalion had been killed by long-range shellfire as far back as Vadenay and Suippes, where they had been detached for duty as town majors.

Renault informed me later that Black, Bunce, and Davis were in the next tent, desperately wounded. I asked for a bathrobe and slippers in order that I might hobble over to see them right away. Davis, unconscious with the ghastly hole in his breast which I had seen on the front, was likely to die at any time. He called for Black in rare moments of freedom from a labored stupor. The appalling sight of Bunce and Black greeted me under the sultry canopy farther down. Bunce's right arm had been amputated below the elbow and he suffered also from six body wounds. Both of Black's legs were off, one of them at the hip. Filled with opiates, still keyed up with a hangover of tension, they talked incoherently and rationally in turns. "A man can stand anything," I thought, horror-struck, as they related the harrowing details of what happened to them.

Bunce said that he had been conscious when Owen and I dragged him from the infernal shack during the bombardment. The shell whose fragments struck me also struck him. He had been hit a third time by shrapnel while lying frightfully wounded in the trench outside. Black mumbled that Redding, already wounded, had been killed by the same shell that had mutilated the narrator's [Black's] legs. He and Wally had been carrying Redding on a litter when it had happened. Wally himself had had a miraculous escape. Black had just learned that he was without legs a few hours before my visit and did not seem to realize what it all meant. I went back to my tent almost ashamed of my own lucky wounds.

A nurse called me to the bedside of Davis later in the day. I limped over laboriously and stood by the gray-faced, heavily breathing boy, who had been through so much with me. I hoped to catch a message which the nurse said he had been trying to convey in lucid moments. He finally opened his dilated eyes, recognized me, and groped feebly for my hand. I took his sweaty, feverish palm in my own. He mumbled confusedly in a mixture of reality and hallucination, bringing a choking lump in my throat. His twisted, pathetic words sank deep. "Mister Thompson, Mister Thomp–son, M–i–s—!" There was a fluttering, gasping sigh. The message, whatever it was, became sealed in death. I hobbled back to my cot in a paroxysm of dumb grief. How much more would a man have to see?

A hospital train pulled up to the siding next day and the mangled contingent of Rainbow wounded rolled away from the bloody Champagne. Across the billowy fields of Marne, beyond Vitry-le-François and St. Dizier, the cars rumbled along a slow and winding route. The bandaged load was disgorged at Bazoille, a few kilometers from Neufchâteau.

Three weeks of rest and daily dressings in one of the wooden barrack wards of Base Hospital 116 was good for healthy wounds. My arm was out of the splint and in a sling. The lost powers of grip due to a slight nerve injury were coming back.

The hole plowed under my shoulder blade by a shell fragment, the slashing cut in the soft flesh over my hip, were filling in nicely. The physical man was convalescing, but the inner man was not doing so well. The blood stains which dyed the memory were not easily washed out. Living and reliving the scenes of dead horses, dead men, and revolting wounds with my battered wardmates may have been natural, but it did one's spirit no good.

Lieut. Marchant, of the First Division, nursed the healing stump of an arm. Capt. Walthall, of the 82nd, a brother of Henry Walthall, of "Birth of a Nation" fame, suffered terribly with a fractured hip, received in the Toul sector.[2] Laughlin, of the Alabama regiment, had a broken lower leg, while Christensen of the Ohio infantry, Jackson, Murphy, and Elliott, of the New York Irish, had arm wounds similar to my own. Delacorte, of the same outfit, nursed a large flesh wound in the thigh. Chaplain Rock, of the First Division, "goldbricking" without shame, admitted that a little war had proved enough for him. Maj. Shiver, of the 82nd in the next cot and Col. Boone, of the 89th just beyond, suffered with mustard gas burns about the face and eyes, received in the St. Mihiel salient.[3]

A group of incoming wounded from the 26th Division brought the talk of war to fever heat. Shambling about in a bathrobe, I seemed drawn irresistibly into the circle of lurid tales. Several of my wardmates were suffering from temporary shell shock. Jerking heads, blinking eyes, agitated nerves became increasingly visible as each gory confab wore on.

Casualty lists in the Paris edition of the *New York Herald* were devoured. Judging from the few familiar names I discovered, the lists were several weeks old. Laughlin found the name of his own brother in one of these scrolls of death. He was inconsolable, almost desperate for a time. A young officer was lugged into the ward a few days later and threw the place into an uproar by stabbing himself with a pair of scissors, swiped from a dressing cart. Capt. Hall and Lieut. Lucas, the medical officers on the ward, gave us the dope on the tragic affair. The "looey" had received bad news from home and had been overcome with overpowering nostalgia.

There were pleasant reliefs from all the mess, of course. Attractive nurses made life seem agreeable and restless at the same time. Music and cards were available at the Red Cross hut. The same gang of men who talked incessantly of their sanguinary experience could usually manage some catcalling banter and humor of a raucous kind. Our medical officers rarely came on the ward without being greeted in chorus by an anthem of multiple parentage and verses too numerous to count.

> *Capt. Hall, he's a great orth–o–pe–dic,*
> *He's really a plumber by trade.*
> *He straightens out bones under ether.*
> *Oh, God, what a mess he has made!*

It took a war and an almost unbelievable chain of circumstances to bring us together in friendship leagues and leagues away.

I was out now, prowling around the world of barracks and tents in a bathrobe or in a nondescript getup, which included Stacy's ragged but precious blouse. Black, Carson, Bunce, Bearing, and several other men from my battalion and company were located in a nearby ward. Having access to the paymaster, which they did not, and having better health, I took these bedridden fellows under my wing. Black and Bunce suffered frightfully, particularly Black, who was compelled to nurse two awful leg stumps. Four men of the 82nd lay naked in the same ward, limbs swollen to twice normal size and bodies splotched with huge blisters from mustard gas. Intermittent showers of bicarbonate of soda from faithful nurses seemed to be the only treatment for the agonized men. The air of the place was fetid, the sights depressing, but I couldn't keep away.

Jim Johnson was my sole link to home. Having moved about with such frequency since spring, it had been weeks since I had received any mail. Headlines in the *New York Herald* blazoned news of the Marines, who for a then unaccountable reason had escaped the rigors of official censorship.[4] All other units, including the Rainbow, seemed to have been swallowed up in an impenetrable void.

Without warning another happy experience developed one bright August day. I was writing a letter home when three nearby figures entered the ward and marched up to my cot. I nearly collapsed upon looking up into the grinning countenance of my cousin, Hugh. "Well I'll be damned. How did you know I was here?" He didn't, was the response, as he introduced me to Maj. Baldwin, the medical officer of his bombing squadron, and to his buddy, Lieut. Anderson. Hugh had seen my name in casualty lists two months before and did not know that I was on my second hospital hitch. Occasionally visiting Bazoille from his station at Gondrecourt, which was close by, he had been accustomed to ask at the hospital if anybody with my name had come in. And, lo and behold, this time there had. He and his friends tried to get Capt. Hall to give me leave for a visit at the squadron headquarters without success. Maj. Baldwin offered to look after my healing wounds and the aviators were told to come back in a week.

It was a long week to wait. Jim Johnson and I killed the first day in Neufchâteau shopping, buying boots and collecting uniforms just finished for us by a French tailor. Neufchâteau! What poignant memories the quaint town induced. There was the Place Jeanne d'Arc, with its statue of the Maid of Orleans, where Tim, Barney, Van, Mack, Sawyer, and I had reviewed marching French and American troops in a remote and snow-blanketed past. Here was the apothecary which the sextet had invaded in search of a cure for Barney's first case of cooties. There was the barbershop, with the bell over the door, where a whole family had turned out to serve us. A small boy had climbed on a box with a vicious razor to torture the massive "Frank Merriwell." What aeons had elapsed since those early days. It was years since Sawyer and Mack had been killed and since that other sorrowful day when Barney had been jerked just as unceremoniously out of my life.

The great day came at last. I was granted a four-day leave and the aviators came back to get me for the promised visit. I piled into the shiny car, which the redoubtable flyers had commandeered. The machine purred away from the cluster of barracks, made the straight road that skirted the banks of the Meuse, and opened up. Maj. Baldwin was at the wheel, with Lieut. Anderson by his side. Lieut. Hugh S. Thompson of the 96th Aero Squadron, and Lieut. Hugh S. Thompson of the 168th Infantry, lounged importantly in the back seat.

CHAPTER FOURTEEN

Home Again

Four days at the headquarters of the 96th Aero Squadron offered a welcome change from the depressing hospital scenes, but only spasmodic relief from persistently intruding memories of the Champagne.

Shortly before I landed at the cluster of barracks and hangars, half-hidden in a grove near Gondrecourt, a group of flyers had buzzed off over the German lines in scout planes and had not returned. A gaunt hole upon the flying field, where a heavy motor had plunged into the earth, bore mute but impressive testimony of a recent crash in which two men had been killed.

The aviators immediately made me feel at home. Most of them had trained with the other Hugh at Issoudun, while several had transferred to the 96th from the La Fayette Escadrille.[1] I was soon a listening member of the crowd, who talked shop around the canteen. I couldn't make heads or tails of the chatter about Handley-Paiges, "crates," windage, Bréguets, three-point landings, etc. On the other hand I could appreciate the references to Quentin Roosevelt, with whom Hugh and his friends had trained, and the news of whose death had lately been reported.[2]

Pat Anderson and Farnsworth had already identified me as the fellow whose wandering Christmas box had been devoured with such relish in a remote past. Along with Hugh and others, they inveigled me into a game of draw poker and I proceeded to contribute further to the upkeep of the Air Service. Jigsaw bits of social rules cropped out amid the cigarette smoke, banter, and clinking chips. Being a cash customer and being firmly rooted to terra firma besides, the local question of I.O.U.'s and their automatic cancellation by certain aerial events did not apply to me, but left me pop-eyed, nevertheless.

Maj. Baldwin, the squadron medical officer, removed healthy scabs from my arm and shoulder wounds in the morning while Hugh, Pat, and Codman looked on, grimacing that the Air Service suited them. On the contrary, after things already seen and heard among the flyers, I was still quite satisfied to take my war, if any, with both feet on the ground.

The squadron prepared for flight in the afternoon. Hugh and Pat stroked a blackbird near the hangars, while the motor was tuned and lower wings loaded with sixteen bombs. I was forced to climb into both cockpits to examine the "crate" which, according to the joking proprietors, was the best in the lot. A red devil framed in a white triangle reposed upon the fuselage of each ship. In one hand the squadron mascot held a bomb ready for delivery upon nether territory. With the free hand the saucy demon thumbed his nose at various and sundry Boches.

The bombers were soon in droning V-shaped flight, after an ear-splitting take-off in swirls of dust.

Maj. Baldwin showed me through the photographic section while they were gone. Walls of a barrack shack were covered with pictorial evidence of damage done to the towns of Conflans and Metz. The flyers returned in a surprisingly short time, squirmed out of gloves, jerkins, and goggled helmets with raucous chatter and invaded the canteen. A few minutes later I was among the audience of mechanics in khaki jumpers who watched a spirited game of volleyball on an outdoor court.

Drizzling rain kept my hosts at home during the rest of my visit. Hugh and I managed a sightseeing tour of nearby Domremy, the humble birthplace of Joan of Arc, before my leave was up. I parted with regret from the hospitable flyers, who took the dangers of their job with such élan. Hugh and Pat commandeered the squadron car and drove me back to the hospital via Neufchâteau and along the Meuse. War meant nothing, if not separation, I thought, when we said good-bye in front of the familiar wooden barracks at Base 116.

I skipped over to see my bedridden friends Carson, Bunce, and Black, right away. Half an hour later, I was adding my voice to those of Jim Johnson from home, Delacorte of the 165th, and the rest of the yodelers, who serenaded the junior medico on the ward:

> *An inventive young wizard, this Lucas,*
> *Who swabs wounds with a beefhanger's touch.*
> *If you don't like his plaster of Paris,*
> *The dam' butcher'll hand you a crutch.*

Life was fluid again in the hospital world of barracks and tents. New patients were coming in from around Nancy and Toul. The old crowd was beginning to break up. Men were being discharged for duty with replacement divisions or combat troops. Others, shattered beyond any chance of further service, were being piled into hospital trains, headed south. Latrine gossip had it that big doings were coming near St. Mihiel. The officers in the ward who had received their mustard gas burns near Seicheprey and Flirey, threw in their knowledge of the "hernia," as the St. Mihiel salient was called by the French.

I soon found a forewarning of more separation upon my pillow. Miss White, a nurse, had brought the message from the ward where my enlisted friends had lain so long in cradles or Balkan frames. Only one of those remaining was able to write. He had no legs, but the rest of the man was intact:

Dear Old Tommy—Am being transferred today at 11:00 they say to Base 8 at Bordeaux. I want to thank you for all your kindness and to let you know that I have come to like you very well—in fact I can't express myself. But you know how I feel. I can't tell you. But good-bye boy & God bless you.
Ever your friend,
Terry Black.

The departure of the mangled trio left a void in my life again and filled me with moody thoughts. It was nearly time for me to be getting back on the job, but the inner wounds, the crimson scars upon the memory, were far from healed. Capt. Hall had said that we could either go to replacement divisions or direct to our outfits when physically fit. What a tortuous dilemma. Somewhere in France was the Rainbow, with Tim, Wally, Perce, and John; with Van and High; with McDonough, Owen, Wickland, and the rest of my platoon. Wherever these priceless friends were, there also was a stack of mail that must have piled up for me during all these weeks. Against a growing yearning to follow the Rainbow again was the safety of the once-despised replacement division at St. Aignan. Why rush to get back into the war? Why not let nature take its course until the memories of the Champagne had thoroughly washed out? After many hours of agonized conflict between reason and desire, my decision was finally made with great reluctance in favor of St. Aignan.

Laughlin hobbled into the ward after supper one evening and knocked these sensible plans sky-high with a joyous bit of news: The Rainbow was gathering in our very neighborhood.

Division headquarters had just been set up at Bournot, hardly twenty kilometers south of us. All rational thoughts evaporated in an impetuous frenzy over the thrilling news. I could not sleep that night for happy visions of the old crowd. Delacorte, of the 165th, who reacted with the same emotions that overwhelmed me, had joined in packing two duffel bags before lunch next day. By night we were armed with ten-day sick leaves to be enjoyed anywhere but in forbidden Paree. The leaves included orders to report to the Rainbow when the furloughs were up. We determined, instead, to make for the outfit, toot sweet. We could sneak off to Paris after we had seen our friends and collected our mail. Little did I suspect that day, when we said farewell to doctors, nurses, and wardmates, that Jim Johnson would get into action again and go by the way of Mack and Sawyer in just a few short weeks.

Delacorte and I hiked to the road that skirted the Meuse and hit the dusty trail, in joyous anticipation of what a few more hours would bring. "Boy, ain't it great to be gettin' home?" An accommodating staff car gave us a lift beyond Harreville and into St. Thiebault. Our eager hobnails made Bourmont just before night. The high plateau upon which the town rested discouraged further punishment for our aching legs. We found a lodging for the night in the valley. French kids hung about the apron strings of our garrulous hostess. An old lady, who looked like Whistler's "Mother," crocheted and rocked in the feeble lamplight.

It was two o'clock when Delacorte and I separated regretfully next day. The hill climb, made in the midst of an August shower, the red tape at division headquarters, and a sumptuous meal at Gen. Menoher's mess had consumed much valuable time.[3] I headed enthusiastically toward regimental headquarters in Blevaincourt, my impotent feet pounding the dusty road under blue skies and creamy clouds. If I'd hurry I'd be with Tim and the bunch before night. Legs ached as I negotiated a series of wooded hills. I was bathed in sweat as my route wound through meadows, orchards, and cultivated fields. The body was growing weak, but the spirit was high in delightful expectancy over the attraction of my goal. A stretch of winding road, lined with sycamores, finally brought me all but exhausted into a quaint town square of tan-colored buildings and roofs of red tile. I flopped on the edge of a rustic fountain for a blow. Recovering my wind, I looked eagerly for familiar faces among a swarm of troops. Reporting in at regimental headquarters in the Hôtel de Ville, I searched the crowds again when I came out. I finally spotted a natty figure who halted at my shout of delight. Gee, it was good to see John and to hear all of the latest dope. He had come over from nearby Chaumont-la-Ville for a large group of replacements, just in. An infuriated mob of veterans, bound for Paris, had just been stopped by sudden orders that had canceled all leaves. Perce, Willy, and Jim Bonner had managed to get away before the gates were closed. "And how's the rest of the gang?" I interrupted eagerly. "How's Capt. Allen?" "Cap" was in the hospital with a touch of gas. Melvin had just come back. Dorsey and Cullen, wounded in the Champagne, Setliffe and Turk, had also just returned. "How about Tim?" I interrupted again, as my fellow "looey" spilled all of the news. John looked at me queerly and finally answered, brows knitted: "Of course, everybody felt terribly about Tim." I experienced a spasm of puzzled alarm. "Why, what's the matter? Is Tim sick?" "No, he isn't sick," John fenced awkwardly. "Has he been wounded?" John continued his faltering, exasperating evasion before giving up a hopeless task. The unavoidable sledgehammer blows were delivered in a soft voice: "I'm awfully sorry, Tommy. I thought you knew. Tim was killed up on the Ourcq." Had I heard right?

"Killed? Tim killed?"

"Yes," continued the sympathetic voice, "on the twenty-eighth of July." The town square reeled about my ears as the devastating truth sank in. I could not speak; could not even ask how Tim had met his death, for the tightening in my throat and for the brick of ice that pressed excruciatingly behind my diaphragm. How stupid of me not to have expected something like this. How terrible that I should have remained in ignorance of the Rainbow for five whole weeks.

John tried to console me as best he could and retired quietly to collect his detail of troops. I headed dazedly and heartbroken for Chaumont-la-Ville. A line of men with rattling mess tins wound toward a rolling kitchen in a barn. Other men supped along the roadside, their backs against cottage and stable walls. Wooden-shoed natives moved among the crowds in mustard brown. A church bell pealed behind me as I carried my sorrow through the mob and beyond the village edge. The unfolding countryside was poignantly beautiful in the waning afternoon. A heavy scent of sweet grass and clover accentuated the indescribable pain. It was six o'clock. A carillon of bells tolled the angelus from Chaumont-la-Ville ahead, from Blevaincourt, and from other villages beyond the adjacent hills. Ah, it may have been the angelus for many, but it was something else for me. How maddening, those reverberating chimes. How bitter to hear Tim's requiem a month late—and all alone on that pastoral road.

I could hardly manage the belated letter that went across

space to Tim's folks. My cup of grief, filled over him, over-flowed when I heard that Van and the redheaded Owen, who had clung to me like a leech in what now seemed to be a happy past, had also "gone west." The remaining details about the Château-Thierry salient sank deep, but without emotional effect. There simply wasn't room for any more than I already felt.

It had taken the Rainbow nine bloody days to push the Boches from the Forêt de Fère, out of Croix Rouge farm, across the Ourcq, beyond Sergy and Hill 212, and out of the Forêt de Nesles. The job had cost frightfully in officers and men. Of the former, whom I knew well, Capt. Moore, Knabe, Albert, Braddock, and Wallace were gone with serious wounds. Among the officers killed were pleasant acquaintances as well as old friends. High had been one of the fellows whom I liked best. Creston had relieved me once in the faraway days of Lorraine, while Irving had come out to the Rainbow with the crowd from the French school. Quillian, the fellow who just knew he would be killed, back there in the days of trenches and Badonviller, was also gone. Only the ghosts of Redding, Zotos, Sharp, Walsh, and others had marched with the battalion from the Champagne to the other battlefield farther west. Only the ghosts of Gross, Hamilton, Anderson, Stock, Cushman, Dunn, Price, and many more had hiked and ridden troop trains from the bleeding salient to the present bivouac in Haute-Marne. I looked unconsciously for squads of familiar faces among the mass of strange ones now filling L company's ranks. McDonough told me in my gloomy billet of Sergt. Holmes, who had been clipped from the head of the marching column by a shell fragment, beyond Le Charmel. Sergt. Runyan had bled to death in the Forêt de Fère from a shell splinter that had severed an artery in the lower leg. He had sat propped in the shoulder straps of his pack, his legs in a road-side drain ditch, while comrades looked after what seemed to be a slight wound. He was sitting in the same position a week later when the depleted company had tramped back over the same ground. Terrific casualties from machine-gun fire had developed at Croix Rouge farm during the advance to the Ourcq and the capture of Hill 212. Brooks, of K company, once lost on the fatal Sawyer patrol, had been drowned while swimming in the Marne, after going through the whole bloody advance.

Perce and Wally, back from Paris with Jim Bonner, unconsciously added to my low spirits; the once swaggering Perce, who now bawled Perry out for saying that Hendricks had been "bumped off" instead of simply saying that Hendricks had died, and the serious Wally, who affected an air of levity, so unnatural to his old self. Disconcerting signs were also evident among some of the platoon. The cultured John and the harum-scarum Jim seemed to be the only old friends who had not changed.

A memorial mass in the church at Blevaincourt on Sunday was followed by a battalion service for the dead. The regimental band played slow music in a grove near Chaumont-la-Ville. Drums beat and Col. Lennert, Col. Townes, and a new chaplain made heartrending talks.

Rumors of early action developed before I was well settled. The St. Mihiel salient was to be reduced and we would play a conspicuous part. The news added lurking fears to my other woes. Why had I ever come back into this mess? Why hadn't I gone to Paris instead of forfeiting my leave?

Battalion maneuvers started with the beginning of a new week. Maj. Bronson, after telling me that I was now a first lieutenant, ordered me to take it easy until my sick leave was up. I tried resting one day in billets, only to learn that I could not bear to be alone. Next morning I got into my old clothes, including Stacy's ragged blouse. Stacy had worn the coveted jacket when he had been fatally gassed and I had been wounded with it on. I'd never let this priceless memento, which had brought me through the Champagne, go now.

I was charging hills against imaginary Boches, at the head of the old platoon, when the afternoon session of maneuvers began. Wally, Perce, Lawson, Wolf, Stradikopulos, and the other old men seemed more like themselves now, but poignant echoes of the past were daily affairs. An early off hour from the physical torture brought a visitor to my billet from Tim's platoon. It was Wilson, a kid who had followed him around, much as the youthful Owen had clung to me. Wilson had dragged the mortally wounded Tim behind a farmhouse ruins, which sheltered other casualties, near the Ourcq. He had remained with his "looey" until the last squads of the platoon dashed out into a rain of machine-gun fire. Meanwhile, Tim had asked Wilson if he thought he was going to die, and the boy, unable to lie to him, had been compelled to answer that he thought he was. "Rainbow" Wilson had come over to tell me about it. He dug a dirty piece of paper from his breeches pocket and handed it to me. I could hardly swallow for the choking lump in my throat. There on the rumpled piece of parchment were Tim's brave, pathetic words, embalmed in Wilson's month-old scrawl: "Tell Hughie to tell the folks I died game." So Tim had thought of me in those last befuddled hours. Even though he had not known where on earth I was, I was still a link to home. No more would I see that comforting form marching with the men of K company. Never again would I hear that galloping laugh.

And the freckle-faced Owen, what of him? Like Tim, his death had not only left me grief stricken, but had shattered my morale as well. Owen had been just young enough for hero worship. I had been eminently convenient, as his platoon commander, and he had seemed to take it out on me. Many had been the time when I had felt uncomfortable, even deceitful, under his blue-eyed gaze. But even more often, I had managed better to hold up my end by striving to live up to his idea of what I was. How could I keep going with these indispensable props gone forever out of my life?

Wally, Perce, and Jim were still on hand. Men of the old platoon were still about, doing their best with the flock of poorly trained newcomers. I'd have to buck up, somehow, if only for their sakes. Cherub was elsewhere with the second battalion now, but Wheeler, a bubbling-over kid much like him, was beginning to take his place. Neither officers nor men could help but make a pet of the boyish "looey" who had not yet seen the front. M and I companies also had new officers who had not been in action. They had recently come in, just as most of the old crowd had been pushed up a grade in rank. Derringer, one of the new lieutenants in K company, seemed morose when I met him at supper in John's billet across the dusty road from ours. John soon explained the cause. Derringer had been married only a few days before he was jerked away from the States and had not had time to receive precious mail. I knew something about that. Hadn't I come back to the outfit and its succession of devastating shocks to learn that a batch of long-awaited-for letters had been forwarded to the hospital, ten days before? I had had no word from home since the remote days of my first hospital tour in Vittel.

Persistent rumors of a forward move turned into more defi-nite news before my forfeited sick leave was well under way, bringing spasms of dread and concern over the new men, many of whom had little or no training at all. It might not even be possible to teach these pathetically dependent wards how to get into their gas masks before the big event. God, would a man really have to lead these raw troops into action—these men who had never even fired their Enfield rifles, which were as strange to officers and noncoms, accustomed to the famil-iar Springfields, as they were to the replacements themselves?[4] The answer came in the form of sudden orders on August 29. We would pull out of Chaumont-la-Ville that night for what was said to be a hike of 235 kilometers to the front. The old familiar bustle and confusion of men, animals, and wagons developed at once. The Rainbow was on the way by 8:30 p.m.

Stragglers among the new men made the going tough. Many were falling behind before the column had made the shadowy town of Robocourt, where natives turned out with lanterns to wish us Godspeed. Then through Sauville and St. Ouen the tramping column wound. More stragglers had made the march an agony of physical torture by midnight. Why had I been such a fool? Why had I come back, when I wasn't fit?

Sulphur dials said 1:30 a.m. when billeting officers led the battalion into a dark open space. Cursing men floundered about in a mixup of animals, rolling stock, and mystifying pup tents. It was three o'clock when Wally and I tumbled into our bedrolls under one of the supply wagons.

We came to, sandwiched between Perce and Sgt. Kling, and crawled out sleepily into the bright sun. The battalion made a gypsy-like medley of men, animals, tents, and smoking kitchens on the edge of a tiny village called Saulxures. Grownups and children who had never seen American soldiers immediately swarmed out to watch us consume slum and stagger about wearily in preparation for another night march. The interested onlookers knew where we were bound, as jabbering comment revealed: "Toul, n'est-ce pas? Ah, oui, San Mihiel, San Mihiel."

We were off by late afternoon to the tune of a familiar chorus, "Bonne chance, bonne chance!" A second endless stretch of murky darkness took us through a succession of shadowy villages to another confusing bivouac upon the open ground. This time we woke up in the fields which surrounded a small cluster of houses, barns, and manure piles called Morlemaison.

Our new bivouac offered the doubtful relief of a four-day halt, during which everything possible was done for the crop of sore feet among the new men. Neighboring orchards were soon tramped flat by the maneuvering second and third battalions, who charged defensive lines of make-believe Boches. The lowly Chink had it right, with his cry of "By God, I'd rather march."

A replacement came through with his version, to bring laughs, which were all too infrequent now: "The calendar says it's Labor Day, but dam' if somebody didn't leave th' calender in th' United States."

Officers scrambled from the shelter of pup tents and wagons to bid for a string of game, peddled by a crowd of native huntsmen, who also knew where willing cooks could be found in town. The whole mob of unkempt doughboys turned out, swarming the crossing of the Gironcourt-Morlemaison roads, when a troupe of Y.M.C.A. entertainers pulled up in a truck. A team of tap dancers clogged upon a platform, brought along for a stage, and a quartet, accompanied by a sad melodeon, harmonized a new song. The ditty spread like wildfire among the troops, temporarily submerging the spasmodic thoughts of the ominous job ahead:

An' I'm gonna get th' other pup,
Th' guy that wakes th' bugler up,

An' spen-n-n-d th' rest of my life in bed.

Catcalling applause had hardly ceased when a crowd of men talked excitedly near the stone wall which backed the fourth platoon's irregular line of ponchos, equipment, and drooping tents. A soldier in a billet across the road had shot himself in the foot. Some said that it was accidental, but those who knew him best said not. New men and officers continued to gossip, wide-eyed over the mess. Open-mouthed replacements gazed stupefied after the disappearing ambulance. Veterans, for the most part, said nothing or grunted: "Th' poor ————."

This, added to my already heavy load of depression, increased my forebodings about the days to come.

We were off again soon after the demoralizing affair. I was getting harder now and we were having less trouble with stragglers, although most of the going was uphill. Hobnails tramped in monotonous rhythm, unaccompanied by talk. I came out of a stupefied trance at each rest, to be haunted by melancholy reminders of Tim and Owen. Black skies began to empty themselves and kept a man from going to sleep on his feet. Deep forebodings returned with a vengeance under the drenching rain. Once upon a time fear had been like the stomach ache, very real when a fellow was cornered with it, but subject to early evaporation after the cause was removed. But now a relentless specter of dread hovered over sopping shoulders as heavy feet splashed on toward St. Mihiel and the bloody calamity that was bound to await us there.

CHAPTER FIFTEEN

Preparation

Myriad hobnails pounded on toward the St. Mihiel salient through alternate stretches of murky darkness and pouring rain. The new men were holding their own, with the aid of veteran comrades, now loaded down with extra rifles and packs.

My anxiety over the job ahead had grown steadily ever since the distracted soldier and his self-mutilated foot had been left behind. Visions of Tim and Owen, thoughts of home, spasms of hope that some miracle might change our course slumbered during endless periods of groggy sleepwalking and came to life with each telescoping halt. Now it was wagons mired on a hill that held us up. Now it was somebody's doubt about the obscure road. Men griped at the end of palsied rests, "What th' hell, we ain't been here two minutes yet."

The solace of tobacco and all other lights were forbidden at night after we had left the misty fields of Battigney. An unexpected shower of priceless mail came to us at Crezilles, amid its surrounding furrows of mud.

My share of long-waited-for news from home consisted of 171 pieces, by the count. Examined hurriedly under the supply wagon tarpaulin, shared with Wally, Wheeler, and two K.P.'s, the packets seemed to have traveled all over France. Jensen, Stradikopulos, Collard, and a group of new men scrambled from nearby pup tents to exclaim over my stupendous haul. Aged papers, filled with war news of a summer now gone, soon littered L company's gypsy-like patch of Meurthe-et-Moselle. My fingers trembled over letters whose chronology was twisted and contents garbled by the passage of months that could never be recalled.

Last things came first, first things came last, things inbetween made little sense. But loving hands had written these very same messages, which I devoured at random and fondled with affectionate care—the hands of June and Dad, of relatives and other friends of Tom, of Ben, whose sole letter revealed that my younger brother had been "somewhere in France" for many weeks. How near, how hopelessly inaccessible Ben seemed. What wouldn't I give just to see him once again?

I had hardly made a dent in the pile of mail before it was time to hit the road for another stretch. Unopened packets went into my mildewed bedroll for consumption when and if ever fate would permit.

The battalion was off in the late afternoon. Pangs of indefinable regret, spasms of foreboding, sprang to life with the sultry, enveloping night. I wrestled with a disturbing bit of news confided by John just before we left. Derringer had received no mail and was terribly downcast as a result. The new officer in K was talking much about death. Distant flashes of artillery and dull thunder added to the all-pervading gloom as my feet dragged along our invisible course. What aeons had passed since I had first seen belching guns at night. What ghastly, lurid memories the ominous spectacle revived.

An endless void of sleepwalking lulled the visions into a jumbled dream. A reeling turn, a buckling halt, brought me to my senses again. Sleepy comment passed up and down the shadowy column. We were lost, it seemed. Rain came down in sheets. Shadowy neighbors griped, "For Christ's sake, why don't they get somebody up 'ere that knows th' road?" The column could hardly walk four abreast on the narrow bypath into which we had been led. We floundered along a winding slope. Rain pattered on my tin hat and ran down my neck. The head of the column seemed to be turning back on its mistaken course. Wagons, animals, and doughboys passed each other in a mystic maze, following wherever the unseen guides were determined to lead. We panted to the top of a slippery hill and wheeled on our path. I company's kitchen, missing a bridge and plunging into a brook, caused an interminable halt. We groped on again through a dark congestion of snorting mules and swearing men. Shouting voices through the rain said that we were stuck for the night. I floundered off the road with the others and sought the shelter of dripping foliage overhead. I fell asleep with my back to the trunk of a tree and came to, teeth chattering, in the gray light of dawn.

Wagons, animals, and haphazard canvas dotted an eerie marsh. Blanketed figures, huddling against bordering trees, shivered, nodded, and stared wide-eyed into the shafts of coming day. The dripping woods came gradually to splashing, mustard-brown life. Grunting men aided quivering mules in retrieving the kitchens from a winding creek. A sleepy mess line wound toward a smoking cooker for shots of hot water, flavored with coffee grounds. The marsh was an incident by 4:00 p.m. Piston-like legs were busy again.

A row of houses, a paved street of Toul, echoed hollowly to our tramping feet, in the falling dusk. A group of gray buildings, an avenue of live oaks, gave way to a shadowy cluster of fortified hills beyond town. These, in turn, gave way to the open road once more. The wind blew in a chilly gale, as night descended upon bobbing helmets in front. Flashes of artillery were smothered by a torrent of rain. Had I ever been dry? Had I ever done anything but pick 'em up and put 'em down in the night? Had I ever been free from this gnawing fear that was akin to physical pain?

Unseen rivulets of marching humanity flowed into the main stream in a rain-drenched town. A jam of trucks, wagons, and machine-gun carts held us up. Invisible men quizzed each other across patches of drizzling ink, "What outfit?"

"Rainbow."

"Same thing, 'Hunnert an' Sixty-eight."

We groped through a turgid maze of squashing feet and rattling wheels. Wally said that we must be in Ménil-la-Tour. No, it was a place called Sancy, another voice assured. The column shuffled forward in a lengthy series of fits and starts. We were winding in and out among stalled trucks and lumbering caissons now, each man hanging on to the man in front. The column worked itself free somehow, obliqued around an overturned truck to the tune of irritable shouts, made an abrupt turn, and mired down in calf-deep mud. Animals fell, wagons were stuck, but the mob of weary doughboys staggered around them and pushed on. Ghost-like trees and a succession of lakes loomed in the coming dawn. Maj. Bronson and Turk splashed up and down the panting line, astride horses, whose legs and bellies were splattered with slime. The column came to a squashing, jerking, bogging halt. We would pitch camp to the right of the road, the major barked, adding that we would stay under cover, whether the rain kept Boche airplanes at home or not. Tardy wagon trains now followed us out of the quagmire and into the bilious light of a dripping forest. Men were prodded into a final spark of second wind for the pitching of tents. An irregular world of canvas came to life amid the sound of thumping artillery and sleepy, "belly-aching" talk, "When do we eat? . . . My dogs is givin' me hell. . . . It ain't you, buddy, it's me."

Leaden skies swept in a steady drizzle upon the Forêt de la Reine. It was the ninth day of September, if fingered calculation meant anything. A conglomeration of men, wagons, ponchos, tarpaulins, tents, water carts, ammunition boxes, and drooping mules was enveloped in an overhanging fog. The gaping maw of a naval gun protruded from a patch of neighboring mist. Squads of L company men, under the dripping trees, scraped mud off of rifles and sodden shoes. The ominous sound of artillery pervaded the tarpaulin shelter, which Wally, Wheeler, and I shared. Talking with them, nibbling at my stack of unfinished mail, moving about among my men, I wondered if others were wearing masks like the one that seemed to be shielding my inner fears. Did Jim and Perce, Beavers and Wolf, Gilbert and Boyd share the nameless dread?

What of the new crowd of Texans and "East Side" men, whose faces were familiar now, if all of their names were not? Even these seemed to have been with us since the early days.

Already subject to fierce attachments, I was beginning to appreciate men as never before. Men like McDonough, Kerberg, and Eaton had been with me through thick and thin. Jim Bonner, who I had once disliked, was now a pal; the cocky Jim, who had boasted of a desire to get into a combat company and who had proved that he had meant it on Hill 212. There was John, over in K, whose well-poised presence was strongly felt; the cultured John, endowed with all of the social graces that went with safety and peace, but who took the war as if it were the natural existence of men. There was the irrepressible, boyish Wheeler, who inspired a proprietary interest in the problems that came up in his platoon. There was Perce, whose vocabulary would make a sailor's parrot blush; the raucous but substantial Perce, who was always on the job. Above all, there was Wally, the conscientious Wally, who put every ounce he had into his little corner of war. I had not thought it possible to feel more deeply, to hold a greater respect for a man, than I had already known for him. But now Wally was Tim, Barney, and Owen all rolled into one.

Gnawing introspection was temporarily downed by work. A variety of duties must be met, whatever a man felt inside. Sore feet must be guided to the sanitary detachment in a nearby clump of woods. A checkup formation must be held. Those men who had never fired their Enfields were commanded to step one pace to the front. Twelve of them did just that. Others, who were not very sure of their rifles, were herded with the first bunch into an unsettled strip of trees, where each man was permitted to fire a clip into the soggy ground at his feet. Sudden orders, during supper, brought ominous thoughts which turned into picturesque language as we struck camp in the rain, plowed to another part of the forest, and pitched camp again.

A new day was as full as the one just gone. Between morning chores, scampering men splashed to the ribbon of mud to watch a fleet of baby tanks churn through the world of tents. Turrets equipped with machine guns and "one pounders" were marked with diamonds, clubs, hearts, and spades. Clanking caterpillars, sputtering engines, left clouds of burning petroleum and a boosted morale in their wake. The iron animals would precede us in the coming assault, if latrine gossip was correct.[1]

A third checkup formation revealed that two of my men had "gone over the hill" in the night. No one knew anything about Parks, but Landers had left word behind; Landers, alias Chink, who received no official pay for his labors, but who had lugged a pack and a rifle through the Lorraine trenches, the Champagne, and the Château-Thierry salient, nevertheless. Chink's message, handed on by an ex-bellhop from Chicago's Loop, brought the first hearty laughs I had heard for many moons. Our man without a country "wasn't in th' army," he had confided. "Nobody couldn't do nothin' to me; I got a belly full of war an' ain't goin' up to no St. Mihiel to get bumped off." The tobacco-chewing Stryker brought more guffaws with a brief but fitting eulogy on Chink's amazing career. "Who said that guy ain't got no sense?"

A battalion officers' meeting reduced my morale to low tide again. The group who pored over elaborate plans and maps in a cluster of supply boxes and wagon tongues emphasized the depleted personnel. Melvin now commanded K; Halsey, I, and Criss, M. Setliffe, Turk, Dorsey, and Cullen were around once more, but over half of the officers were new and had not been in action before.

The major's maps offered a general picture of what the St. Mihiel salient meant, but points like Pont-à-Mousson, Apremont, Mont Sec, and the plains of Woëvre meant little to me. A narrow section of the salient's southern face, however, was something else again. The Rainbow would be in the center of the Fourth Corps on the coming advance. We would push toward the first day's objectives, regardless of the progress of the First and 89th divisions on our left and right. Our battalion would be the spearhead in the regimental assault. L and M companies would go over in the first wave, followed by K and I and in turn by our second battalion. The division would jump off from trenches between the towns of Seicheprey and Flirey and would be expected to reach a rough line drawn through Nonsard and Thiaucourt before night. A thick woods, infested with two lines of entrenched Boches, a third line beyond that, the town of Essey, and a small tributary of the Moselle lay between our jumping-off place and the first day's goal. The towns of Beney and St. Benoit, a part of the Hindenburg Line,[2] separated the first halting place from the salient's base, the ultimate goal. The 89th Division occupied the trenches from which we would depart. Details from our first battalion would go ahead to familiarize themselves with the sector at the proper time. These would lead us in as the 89th moved over to the right to make room for us. The group who listened to Maj. Bronson would dress just like the men, with no distinguishing mark of rank. D day and H hour might come at any time and we would keep the men under cover until ordered to pull out for the front. The major's instructions were followed by a study of artillery timetables, airplane signals, and the missions of supporting auxiliary arms.

I left the meeting deep in ominous thought, despite the tabulation of airplanes, tanks, mortars, and heavy guns. The sound of distant artillery meant but one thing; calamity with a capital C. A man was asked to plow through ten kilometers of mud to a gallows that marked the end of the trail. He would ascend the steps of his own volition, adjust the noose around his own jugular, and spring the trap when a sulphur dial pointed to a given o'clock.

Those who splashed through the woods by my side seemed normal enough. What was the matter with me, I wondered? Was I just a plain coward? I tried to be easy on myself. Perhaps I would not feel this way if I had not been hit by flying slugs of iron in that cauldron of July. I had come back to the outfit too soon, that was it. Maybe I had gazed too often and too long upon Black's ghastly leg stumps and other revolting hospital scenes. Well, whatever happened to me, I had traveled with some real men, men whom I couldn't let down.

A restless night. A soul-searching morning. Wally and I were back under our shelter of canvas again. I attacked my remnant of mail in an effort to lift the lurking pall. I brushed the handful of letters aside when my usually reserved bunkmate developed a talkative streak. His father had died when he was nine. He had been the man in the family since. He knew that he would get his up front and he did not see how his mother and his sisters could get along without him. Faraway women who had been only names before became flesh and blood people as Wally revealed himself. I scoffed at his forebodings without succeeding in banishing my own. Look at all he had been through in the past. What about that narrow escape he had in Champagne? My feeble efforts were of no avail. Wally was as calm about it all as he was convinced, I discovered as we threshed the whole thing out. What a difference between Wally and me.

I was concerned about my own skin, but his thoughts were wandering along an entirely different talk. Even in that hour of anguish I knew that I had seen the very insides of a man, a man who could go out there and face it all thinking only of others and not caring one whit about himself.

Perce and Wheeler splashed up to our tarpaulin with the throat-tightening news that we would pull out for the front at 9:00 p.m. I seemed to stop breathing when the rich baritone added that five o'clock next morning was the hour that had been set. A familiar scurry followed the dreadful news. Watches were synchronized at a final meeting of the battalion officers. Two sandwiches apiece, 250 rounds of ammunition were issued to the men. Canteens were filled from water carts and bags. Tents were struck in a drizzling rain, while cooks prepared for an early supper of coffee and slum. Packs were rolled and stacked in the woods, to be guarded by a man from each platoon. A blanket apiece would be carried into the calamity to come. These duties finished, I made a packet of money and trinkets to be turned over to Sergt. Kling, while Wally, Wheeler, Perce, and Jim did the same.

I turned to a last handful of letters again, in an effort to keep from dwelling upon what lay ahead. I read several of these without taking the contents in, while Wally scanned the few papers I had saved. Others I destroyed in a fit of hopeless despair. Two or three went into the pockets of the ragged blouse which had belonged to poor Stacy before it had come to me. A weather-beaten envelope, its facings obliterated by numerous forwarding scrawls, caught my eye. A great light dawned and I slit the faded seal. I devoured the message, which dropped with such strange, poignant cheerfulness into my miserable world. I read it aloud to Wally, who sat tailor-fashion under our tarpaulin flap:

Hello Hughie A hasty line to the address that's supposed to be yours. Am anxious for word from you to back up the good news just heard from Wally and Perce. "Cap" inquires of you and Barney, as do all of the bunch in K.

Yesterday's mail brought a flock of letters from home and from the girl (it's a grand and glorious feeling). News from over there is all good and the service stars increase daily, helped along somewhat by a device called the selective draft. Jim Green seems to be the only one of our old cronies who remains immune to the "breeze."

I suppose ere now Perce has written that we are in Champagne, wherever that is. They are expecting big doings here and we will receive same with the customary vim and vigor, you can bet your francs on that.

Well, Hughie, my best always, and here's to Der Tag, when you get back to One Hundred and Sixty-eighth.

As ever,   Tim

What a flood of memories the message from beyond brought in its wake! What a medley of feelings the cheerful words stirred under my ribs. Alas, Der Tag had come again. I had come back to 168th and to what? And now, I might be with Tim before the end of another day. If only I could meet the issue as he had done—"Tell Hughie to tell the folks I died game."

The battalion plowed through the clinging mud, drenched by a downpour of rain. Floundering through the darkness with Wally and McDonough at my side, my memories, my gnawing fears, my straws of hope tumbled over each other in a cascade of muddled, anguished reverie. Thoughts of June and Dad; thoughts of Tim and his message which rested over my left breast; thoughts of the untrained men who splashed along in front of us; thoughts of the gray-green figures who waited for

us somewhere ahead in the night. The whole lurid kaleidoscope slumbered after several kilometers of mud and another
stretch on firmer ground. The muffled ca-rump of shells re-
kindled the fires of my befuddled dreams. What would morning bring? What if the Boches should throw a terrifying avalanche of artillery down upon us, as they had done in
Champagne? What if they should overwhelm us in mortal
combat.

The column staggered on for ages before coming to a jerky
halt. Shadowy buildings loomed through the rain and gave
way to an invisible mob, which jammed a narrow street. The
smell of dank manure, the noise of scraping feet, lumbering
vehicles, and sputtering trucks filled the murky gloom.
Mounted horsemen tried to untangle the invisible maze. The
voices of French refugees came from the top of rattling carts.
Other voices spanned thin patches of the soupy darkness.
"What outfit, buddy? . . . "
"Rainbow! . . . Third Division over here."

We had wormed out of the black, panting congregation of
Mandres now and were on the open road again, stumbling
around treacherous, water-filled shell holes along an indigo
course. Projectiles of large caliber whistled angrily and ended
in muffled "booms." A "155" screamed close. We scattered into
the dark fields and fell flat, under a flaming, banging crash.
The march was resumed through damp, acrid smoke. Streaks
of lightning brought a crossroads into shuttle-like relief. An
overturned cart and an animal lay in our path. A man groaned
in a sickening pool near the ditch. "Jesus, God!" someone
gasped hoarsely, in the night.

CHAPTER SIXTEEN

St. Mihiel

Shells whirred and wailed above the water-logged ditch, where I huddled with Wally, Wheeler, and Jim. "Seventy-fives" barked, almost on line with us. Far-off machine guns chattered dully, in angry fits and starts. Exhausted men slept at our feet, oblivious to the noise and rain. Gray-green specters seemed to peer through the rumbling gloom; gray-green specters who waited, waited; waited for us to come. What were they like, these men whom we must kill? Were they like the others I had seen, or were they the huge, formidable men which my anguished imagination seemed to paint? Would I kill them or would they kill me? The thought brought an overwhelming wave of misery at the dreadful prospect of five o'clock. "No reprieve," I muttered. "No reprieve from the punishment of five o'clock."

A "77" screeched above the cannonading, a blinding flash threw us flat. Jumpy nerves had hardly settled into gnawing anxiety again, when a husky voice breathed in my ear. Perce wanted us right away. We scrambled to our feet and followed Perce through the slippery trench. Boche shells streamed low overhead toward the carmine lightning that fringed the blackness in our rear. McDonough and Lawson hissed in recognition as we passed, stumbling over unseen figures who sprawled under our sucking feet. The eyes of other men seemed to pierce the mantle of darkness that shrouded their faintly visible tin hats. . . . We splashed by a shadowy mortar

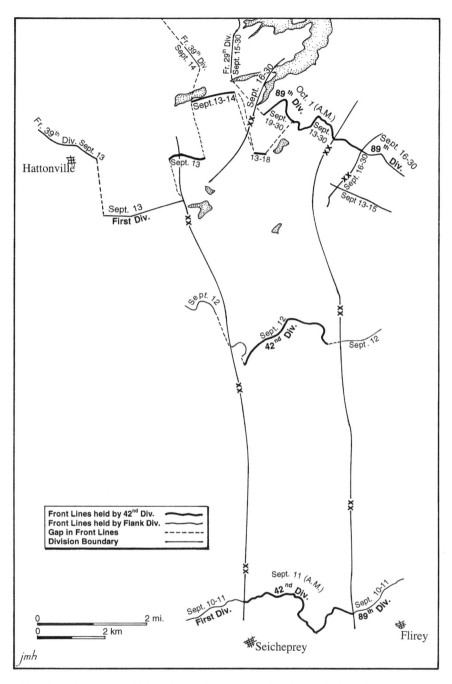

The front lines, St. Mihiel, September 12, 1918. Map by John M. Hollingsworth.

crew, through a mystic maze of trenches, ducked under a blanketed entrance and groped down a narrow stair. Thumping artillery grew softer in the dripping candlelit shelter. A muffled thud shook the timbers of its filthy bunks, a gust of air fanned the sickly flame.

Perce's prominent features, surrounded by a villainous growth of beard, were ghostly in the feeble light. With my fellow "looeys" I crouched near, waiting for him to speak. How often I had witnessed such a tableau underground. What strange illusions wove themselves around the eerie scene. It was all a dream; a nightmarish dream, this business of five o'clock. We had gone back to the beginning of things, that was it; back to the trenches of Badonviller, which we had left in a dark and distant past. Perce's baritone broke my spell of reverie. We would deploy in half-platoons when we had cleared our wire, I heard in a muddled daze. We must hug the barrage that would drop in front of us at five o'clock. Remember, it was nearly half a mile to the Bois de la Sonnard and the first line of "krautheads" we must rout out of the woods. Talbott's platoon of K would mop up for us with bombs, while M.P.'s would handle all the prisoners we could grab. We must shove on through the woods, "knockin' off" as many of the ————s as we could see. The voice asked a question now. Whose platoon was next to the 89th Division, on our right? Wheeler was already in touch with K company of the 356th. Well, he was to maintain liaison with our neighbors as long as they kept pace with our advance. The boy officer, who had never been in action before, was traveling with the best platoon commanders in the A.E.F., I heard in a paroxysm of thrilling pain. He would hold up his end of things, Perce knew, and Wheeler's eyes shone with excitement in response to the throat-tightening words. How lucky he was, I thought, not to realize the full significance of five o'clock.

"Five o'clock." The crushing weight hung like a pall over the bluffing words of Jim, who griped about our lack of wire cutters and bombs; over Perce's sarcastic rejoinder that maybe Gen. Pershing would call off the war until Jim got fixed; over Wally's grin at the sepulchral repartee.

"Five o'clock." I mumbled the bizarre phrase as we climbed the stairs and groped into the rumbling night again. It had stopped raining when we floundered past Young and his mortar crew. One of our "heavies" had landed in an ammunition dump behind the German lines and streaks of red tinted the sky above the lapping flames. Clanking caterpillars and sputtering engines sounded about the funereal shells as we splashed off to instruct our noncoms about five o'clock.

McDonough and Lawson herded my corporals near the lane in the wire, through which the fourth platoon would depart. I would take the squads of Beavers, Nelson, Getty, and Wolf, advancing with the latter group myself. McDonough would follow with the rest, while Gilbert and Jensen would advance behind my skirmish line to keep anyone from falling out. McDonough had better have Collard and Stradikopulos do the same for his half-platoon. Further instructions imparted, I groped among the shivering replacements, their helmets barely visible in the pinkish glow. What a bluff I carried, with my words of synthetic cheer. We'd give the Boches unshirted hell before the sun came up.

Wally, Wheeler, and Jim finally sloshed down the trench and we settled in a teeth-chattering huddle to wait for five o'clock. Feverish thoughts seared my tired brain as Jim driveled in bluffing falsetto above the swishing of shells; thoughts of Barney, Owen, and Tim; thoughts of my mother, who had died in a world that no longer seemed to exist; thoughts of John and Derringer, of Dorsey, Setliffe, and Cullen, who huddled somewhere off to our left and rear; thoughts of the Boches who waited in the trenches of the opposite woods. Sulphur dials were consulted nervously amid the awe-inspiring noise. A thousand times I felt of the chin strap of my helmet, of the gas mask on my chest, of the "45" that hung like a lead weight from my hip. "Three fifty-one . . . three fifty-eight . . . four o'clock," the minutes ticked off. "Four six . . . four eleven." A "77" screamed close. We sprawled in the trench bottom under a shower of water and mud. A man gasped, terrified, above our heads. "Four sixteen . . . four seventeen": gray-green phantoms haunted our rendezvous again, chattering guns seemed to transmit the desperate feelings of unseen men. I tried to whip myself into a fury of hate, but hate simply would not come to relieve the gnawing fear. "Four thirty-five . . . four thirty-eight"; time was fleeting, fleeting toward the end. Would the suffocating burden never lift? "Four forty-two . . . four forty-four . . . four forty-five." We struggled to our feet. My throat tightened, icicles ran up and down my spine as I felt for the muddy hands of Wally, Wheeler, and Jim. I whacked soggy backs and felt thumps on my own light pack. "See you in Essey," barked Jim, above the swishing shells. "Good luck, good luck," from Wally and Wheeler, who splashed off to their respective platoons on my left and right. The voices called like weird sirens, as I stirred about, shaking men from heavy sleep. "See you in Essey," an echo murmured, as I climbed into a silhouette of posts and wire, with the glistening bayonets of Wolf's squad at my back. "Four fifty-four . . . four fifty-five." My insides quivered, my head swam, I stumbled into a tangle of pricking wire, with apparitions foundering in my wake. "Four fifty-seven . . . four fifty-eight." "Good luck, good luck," the voices rang. . . . "Five o'clock." A spontaneous beam of light flickered along the front. I staggered forward, heart in mouth, my ears ringing with bell-like sounds. "Good luck, good luck, good . . ." The night ahead turned inside out with a volcanic, belching roar.

I stumbled toward the boiling cauldron, muttering a frenzied prayer. The effort died when I fell into an abandoned trench, floundered out into an octopus of wire, and tore myself loose with frantic jerks. Groping figures followed through more grasping tentacles and through hellish furrows of clinging mud. Grotesque shadows deployed in the dazzling lights. Someone yelled through the terrific noise: "Keep your three-yard interval," and I suddenly realized that the voice belonged to me.

The line took up its march behind a curtain of smoke and flame. Conscious only of the nearest men, I cleared a stretch of upturned mud under a deluge of bursting shells. Choking fumes mingled with a sickening stench as we plowed across more treacherous ground and ascended a bombarded slope. A ghastly tongue of fire licked bobbing heads to the right. There was a muffled shriek and Wolf's squad swerved over through a zephyr of concussion to fill the yawning gap. A hundred yards, a mile, ten miles, through screaming detonations and we reached an erupting crest. Literally drunk with awe, I seemed to float over the summit and into the fountains of spewing phosphorous, which brought waves of burning heat.

On, on I floated, hardly conscious of the woodpeckers, whose "rat-tat-tat" hammered dully above the terrifying shells. The barrage crept down the hill. I floated on in a fantastic trance, unmindful of the angry wasps that droned past my ringing ears. A line of brown wormed forward irregularly, under the sepia glow of innumerable parachute flares. Maxims chattered, Chauchats barked through the flashing lights. Festoons of varicolored rockets shot through the golden smoke. What was all the tumult about, I wondered, as someone fell in a drove of buzzing wasps? Where was I, anyway? Was I still alive or had I already been wafted to another world? Clusters of red and yellow now sprayed heavenward against a background of bilious green. Raging night turned into sickly, chattering day. Frantic machine guns jerked me from my dreams and into a state of goose-pimply fear. Wooly thoughts raced madly between bursts of fire from a rim of trees; seconds were ages, as my surroundings and their implications sank in. The barrage pounded in the German wire and moved into the trees, leaving saffron clouds in its crashing wave. We must storm the Boches without its aid. Men lay scattered in the mud and stubble to my left. A group huddled farther on, behind an overturned tank. Squads wormed forward through abandoned trenches on the right. "Seventy-sevens" and Minenwerfer banged down the slope.[1] I bolted forward with Wolf's squad and fell into a smoking hole. We waited for breathless ages, it seemed, for more men to come up on line with us. I raced frantically to our left rear to prod a terrified group of new men who would neither advance nor lie flat.

Somebody was rushing up and down the line farther to the left, while Wally's men appeared and vanished in a clump of smoking underbrush. I dashed back to Wolf and scurried to the right, shouting for scattered groups to guide us on. I fell flat among a group of replacements, who gasped that Wheeler had been hit. A handful of men crawled toward us through a patch of weeds. Between angry bursts from the woods, one of the strangers introduced himself, as though we were meeting on a city street. Simpson was his name, from Enid, Oklahoma, and the 356th. Could his squad fight with us?

Dashing back to Wolf, when advancing men to the left attracted the angry gun, we made a rush for the cover of smoking holes. Shells pounded dully now, deeper in the woods. The unseen gun, which seemed to be well behind the first visible parapets, hammered desperately at our every move. Other Maxims chattered along the fringe of floating smoke. A rush under a shower of bursting shells. A dash through the stubble and mud. The guns were chattering like mad. All thought of controlling the scattered line gave way to fearful self-preservation. We'd be killed if we lay still. There was a gambling chance if we charged ahead.

"Rat-tat-tat-tat!" came the mad staccato from the ghostly trees. We bolted to the edge of upturned posts and wire. Wolf called that we would make it, the "put-put-put" of his automatic rifle succeeding his muffled words. A mad dash to a shallow gully in the demolished barricades; Gilbert fell forward in a grotesque salaam, knees and head in the mud, blood streaming from the side of his face. . . ."Put-put-put . . . ."

"Rat-tat-tat-tat!" The Maxim drowned the barking Chauchat out. Closer, closer we drew to the smoking trees, worming, crawling, and firing into the terrifying sounds. Someone was hit and beat his fists into the mud as I ducked under a rain of pinging missiles. The figure lay still, when I looked up, heart in mouth. A frenzied scramble through patches of broken wire. Streaks of gray darted from a barricade of mud and iron and made for a fire trench, one of the Boches plunging in a crumpled heap, "Rat-tat-tat-tat . . . rat-tat . . . ." Stradikopulos fell, men dropped flat in a blur of brown, Wolf dived headlong into the twisted debris, a few paces to my left front. His Chauchat catapulted into the mud ahead as I covered my face with my arms. Seconds, ages. I crawled toward the discarded gun, icicles pricking my spine. I watched as if mesmerized as Wolf fluttered like a beheaded pullet, flopping first on his back and then on his face again. Mud splattered before my eyes, missiles rattled in Wolf's tin hat. The firing sprayed off to the right, into a wave of moving brown.

Wolf lay still as I squirmed toward him, firing my "45" at a glimpse of gray, which appeared and vanished above a strand of wire. Figures in brown rushed up on the left, bringing the vicious staccato and the sickening rattle in Wolf's helmet again. Planes howled aloft. I crept a yard, I crept two, now abutted by other crawling, firing men.

A missile tugged at my sleeve. A red-hot slug crushed the bones of my middle, pitching me into a pile of mud and rusty wire. In spite of the horrible realities, there was a flashing instant of dumb surprise. I tried desperately to drag myself into a shell hole, which someone left. I sank into a cold sweat of agony, a broken leg askew. "Rat-tat-tat-tat!" hammered the fiendish gun, bringing the sickening, metallic sounds. The firing sprayed off to the left. Terrific pain, deadly fear, fought for supremacy under the droning planes, the clicking sounds and glimpses of rushing men. A streak of doughboys brought the terrifying staccato again. God. It was the end, it was the end. If only I could say a last word to someone. If only . . . "Rat-tat-tat-tat . . . rat-tat-tat . . . rat-tat!" The loud firing ceased, guns chattered from the distant left, a strange pounding, a desultory fire sounded deeper in the woods. Muddy, stumbling figures vanished over the German parapets, bullets pinged overhead. I lay breathless for ages in a mingled agony of terror and pain. Gray-green blurs moved out of the smoking void, into which the doughboys had disappeared. More doughboys and Boches passed in a swirling haze. My head buzzed, my back felt crushed, hobnails and heavy boots passed in a bedlam of unintelligible sounds. Phantom voices rang in my buzzing ears: "Five o'clock, five o'clock."

"Good luck, good luck."

Far away artillery and popping musketry sounded beyond the mantle of smoke that enveloped the Bois de la Sonnard. Planes droned overhead and dissolved above the strangely peaceful trees. Tanks sputtered, their caterpillars spinning desperately somewhere off to the rear. A column of reserves wound like a snake to my left and wriggled into a neck of the woods. The pain in my back had settled into a surging ache, which changed to spasms of agony if I moved at all below the hips. Relief, overwhelming relief from the fear of mangled death dominated even the shooting pains. It seemed hours since the heavy firing had ceased and since gray and brown figures had untangled themselves from the hazy blur in front. It was hours since a group of doughboys had stopped with a haul of frightened Boches to lift my helmet and rake the pricking strands of barbed wire from under my arms and chest. I had thought it midafternoon and had worried for fear that stretcher-bearers would not pick me up before night. One of the men had shoved Wolf's riddled musette bag under my broken hip and moved off into the bright sun, leaving me with the bewildering news that it was eight o'clock.

The sun came out full force and baked down upon the back of my neck. The dead Boche ahead sprawled in an enticing oasis of shade. A camouflaged gun emplacement, a fallen tree, was visible beyond the gray humped form. Wraithlike clouds of vapor floated from the damp clothing of Wolf and of the other crumpled men who lay about. "Water, water," I called weakly, trying with painful contortions to get at the canteen which was just out of reach in the middle of my aching back. My throat was like cotton under the streaming sun. "Water, water," I called at sight of brown and gray figures, who moved along the muddy heaps. "Water, water," I gasped as a group of Boches with stretchers followed a doughboy into the wire to examine one of the still figures and to lift another upon a stretcher and disappear. I continued to signal at each glimpse of the prisoners, who had been pressed into service as stretcher-bearers. "Water, water," I called for the thousandth time, when one of the crumpled dead came to life with a groaning stir. Stryker squirmed toward me, his face ashen and muddy, a purplish stain soaking through the sleeve of his heavy coat. There were painful tugs at my middle. At last, the warm, precious liquid gurgled down my parched throat.

Stryker emptied the last dregs in his own mouth and lay still at my side, a jagged, crimson hole in the palm of an out-stretched hand.

During measureless time I lay aching under the steaming sun. Four frightened Boches appeared with Boyd and lugged Stryker away. Other Boches carried wounded high on shoulders from my restricted view. Boyd returned after thirsting ages. I sucked a canteen dry and prepared for the ordeal of moving, while Boyd identified Wolf, Stradikopulos, Perry, and a new man, who lay dead to my left and right. Even the Boches, whose heavy feet and shoddy pants surrounded me, seemed to know just what I wanted them to do by way of help. Boyd's bayonet and wire cutters were used to rake me free from prick-ing debris. He removed the musette bag from under my limp leg, while a German held the hip up with his hands. When Boyd lifted the leg ever so slightly, another kneeling Boche shoved the litter underneath. A third, holding my belt in the back, grunted "langsam, langsam," in chorus with Boyd's "easy, easy," and I lowered myself on the stretcher face down, the inner side of my broken leg, from knee to heel, resting on the precarious stretcher edge.

Shells and musketry sounded faintly above the buzzing in my head, when I was lifted on shoulders for the painful trek across no man's land. The stretcher tilted, bringing a spasm of pain and a death fear of falling. I gasped for a halt and was lowered to the mud again. Boyd went off with a diminutive Boche and came back with one who was more nearly the size of the other three. The ghastly trek was resumed, the Boches struggling through the wire and abandoned trenches, past the muddy forms of several dead, through the slippery stubble, and over more upturned earth. The wide-eyed Germans spoke to me in guttural commiseration at each panting rest, while Boyd recounted that Kerberg, Beavers, Stock, Lawson, and Gilbert were among the killed. Some of the new men, "th' poor ————s," had scattered all over hell and "beaucoo" platoon commanders and sergeants had been "bumped off." They had had to run around in the firing trying to keep the advancing lines under control. Matters had been made worse when several corporals had been knocked out. The second battalion had suffered lightly. The stiff resistance by the Boches had given way after the onslaught of L, K, I, and M companies, which had broken the first line of "krauthead" trenches. By 6:30 the advancing troops had begun to push on at breakneck speed.

Another painful jogging toward the rear was followed by a panting rest. Still another trek and rest brought the Germans to puffing "chews." They wiped their sweating faces with shoddy sleeves as they sat near my head grunting with fatigue. "Schwer, schwer," they panted, intonation saying plainly that I made a heavy load. Boyd continued his incoherent account of the morning, the lurid details leaving me emotionally cold. At last I was deposited under a clump of trees, where men groaned and talked hysterically beyond my limited vision. A familiar voice apologized for having hurt me and I found myself gritting my teeth and gasping in pain, under the excruciating process of being lifted from my belly to my back. I looked into the wan face of Maj. Branch. A man with a Red Cross brassard held my broken leg high and taut, while another cut the hobnail shoe from the swollen foot. Still others ripped me free of sidearms, overcoat, and bloody pants, while the major cut the sleeve of my blouse for shots of antitetanus and morphine. Was my back broken, I quizzed anxiously, between gasps of pain? No. Then why couldn't I move my uninjured leg? I had a mighty bad fracture, I heard through the buzzing vertigo. The other leg would come around O.K. A splint was painfully applied and a bandage taped over a ghastly bullet hole near the groin. I winced in an agony of cold sweat when the leg was strapped heavily with adhesive and stretched taut toward the end of the splint. The savage contraption finally propped high on a folded overcoat and the opiates taking effect, I became conscious of the grim scene in the woods. Frightened Boches of all descriptions huddled under the trees. A doughboy prodded others with a menacing bayonet and a column of prisoners stumbled to the rear, some of them helping others along. One of the bandaged wounded hobbled off, using a whittled tree limb for a crutch. Stretchers with gory loads were moving out of the woods, while others were being lowered to the undergrowth and mud. The group of Germans who had carried me off the field were more at ease now, apparently free of their first fears of what might happen to them at the hands of muddy captors. A flaxen-haired youth, crouching close to me and looking like a frightened deer, made a peace offering from the contents of his pockets. Postcards, a knife, and a silver pencil were dropped on my blankets, while another prisoner gave me buttons from his shoddy jacket. Gray-faced wounded, sucking cigarettes nearby, conversed with a Boche noncom, who informed them in broken English that most of the prisoners were from the 6th Grenadiers of the 10th Division. "Kaiser think he win—not me," he blurted with a woebegone shake of the head, when asked what he thought of the war.

Hazy movements began to develop before my dopey eyes. Setliffe, with a crimson bandage about his naked chest, Gibbons and Turk with gunshot wounds in the arm, an unrecognizable figure badly wounded in the face, were lifted high by the struggling Boches. Williams, Getty, Nelson, and Collard; old and new men from the other platoons; unknown wounded from K, I, and M waited patiently to be moved, groaning, smoking or mumbling over the dreadful events that had happened since five o'clock.

Maj. Bronson, Criss, Varn, and Halsey had been hit early in the advance. Smith, of the machine-gun company, and Young, of the mortars, were dead. Senses drugged, emotions stretched to the breaking point, I could not absorb the grotesque news that Derringer, Cullen, and Dorsey had been killed, the first by high explosive and the others by machine-gun bullets in the body and in the top of the head. Dazed brain and quivering insides fought unsuccessfully over the grim assurances that the muddy legs and riddled overcoat, half-hidden by a blanket, near the foot of a tree, was all that was left of Wheeler.

It must be true, muddled reason said, that Wally had been hit in the breast by a slug of high explosive, had sent back word that his line was moving up, and had staggered on for an unbelievable distance before falling dead.

"Wally dead?" My warped emotions tried to take the fact in. Wally, the pal to whom I was even more fiercely attached than to the others. Why, if Wally were dead, I would be grief-stricken, and here I was feeling nothing except a sickening vertigo, a dull pain in the back, and a vague sense of relief that I would never go into battle again.

I was riding high on shoulders now, powerful drugs twisting fact and fancy in a tangled web. "Dorsey, Wheeler, Cullen, Stock, Gilbert, Kerberg, Lawson, Wolf." Names and visions, visions and names rushed through my giddy head. A line of Boches and heavy litters wormed out of the Bois du Jury. Over duckboard ramps and rustic bridges the quartet of panting Germans carried me and my aching back. "Dead, dead; Wally dead." The fantastic words beat in cadence with each jogging rise and fall of the precarious litter. Through a winding trail in the woods, over abandoned trenches, past a battered dug-out, the snake-like line twisted under the trees. Through a maze of reserves, who stumbled by in a narrow path, and I was at last lowered to the gutter of a congested road. Marching troops, rattling caissons and machine-gun carts, sputtering ambulances passed in a bewildering blur. Three unknown doughboys groaned inside the ambulance, to which I was lifted by the forms in shoddy gray. The sounds of heavy traffic continued to fill the world outside. Scraping feet, chugging trucks, muffled the faraway musketry and the cursing voices that prodded intractable mules. Even the surging pulsations in my aching hip seemed to have the quality of sound themselves. "Gangway, gangway, for ambulance," someone yelled, causing me to hold on tight in anticipation of an agonizing jerk. "Auf wiedersehen," throaty voices sounded near my ringing ears, while bell-like sirens murmured above the perplexing din: "Five o'clock, five o'clock."

"Good luck, good luck . . . good luck."[2]

CHAPTER SEVENTEEN

The End

Six months. Six endless, agonizing months since that fatal day in September when I had come out of the St. Mihiel salient with my own life, but without many more comrades whose places could never be refilled; six months that were sometimes blurred, sometimes vivid, but always fantastic, before I exchanged the hell of Base Hospital No. 48 for the now relative heaven of Base Hospital No. 69.

Long accustomed to my own fetid wound, I hardly noticed the odor of bandages, dressings, and Dakin's solution which permeated the somber officers' ward. Capt. Douglas, a fracture case on my right, and Keenan and Bartell, bathrobed patients with heavily splinted arms, played red dog on the captain's bed. A medical officer and nurse probed the pleural cavity of a gasping emphysema case across the way. Sisters of Charity, from that part of Brittany which surrounded the hospital, visited among the pallid men to my left, while a group of bedridden fractures beyond serenaded an inspecting medico with an oft-repeated local version of "Dublin Bay":

> *Good-bye, I'm on my way*
> *From dear ol' Savenay—*
> *I do not care to stay,*
> *That's why I'm feeling gay.*
> *The doctors all agree*
> *It's fun to ? on me.*

> *That's why I'm glad to get away*
> *From Savenay.*

The choral farewell, which was a bit premature, to say the least, had hardly died away when a group of "Y" entertainers shoved a portable melodeon into the ward. Patients raised up on elbows for the performance, while Stevenson, with a leg off above the knee; Fleming, with both legs off at the hips; and other wheel-chair cases rolled under their own hand power toward the source of excitement. A uniformed organist struck a few sickly chords; a quartet of varied abilities burst into song:

> *In the good old summertime,*
> *In the good old summertime,*
> *Strolling down that sha . . .*

The singers were interrupted by a series of feeble catcalls and the eastern end of the ward offered its interpretation of the ancient portable hit:

> *In th' base at Savenay,*
> *Where th' sick an' wounded lay*
> *Runnin' up their temper'tures,*
> *More an' more each day.*
> *Oh, they put 'em all in plaster casts*
> *An' that's a very good sign*
> *That they will stay in Savenay*
> *Till th' good ol' summertime.*

"Oh, Frenchy," "Smiles," and "Hinky, Dinky, Parlay Vous?" followed in raucous succession and the song leaders pushed their music box to another part of the building.

Only the initiate could know that the emaciated yodelers who now settled down into grimacing moans or grunting talk had exercised their vocal cords not because they were particularly happy, but out of sheer gratitude that they had lately left a past which had seemed a hell on earth for their mutilated but relatively comfortable present.

Although my own circumstance was just one of hundreds and rather cause for thanks, compared to that of many others, I understood it best, aided by that seemingly natural egotism which makes one's little personal world—especially in adversity—the most important world of all. I knew that I might still lose my leg, after a fight of many weeks to save it. I knew that the future held more months upon my back and a series of operations, when and if ever I reached the United States, but for the moment I was in no mood to anticipate these painful events. Like most of my wardmates I was thankful that nature had at least turned compassionate for the nonce, leaving only manageable traces of those six months such as a plaster cast with a "window" that permitted the daily dressing of my festering wound; a temperature that rarely exceeded 102 degrees; paroxysms of rheumatic pain from my injured sciatic nerve, which were now as much a part of me as breathing, and a few other routine indignities better left undescribed. Only recently had I been taken down from a Balkan frame, incased in plaster and shipped by stages from Base No. 48 to Base No. 69.

The last lap of the journey, made from Nantes to Savenay in a bumpy ambulance, had angered the streptococci, which thrived upon the bones and tissues of my hip. The microbes had called in swarms of reserves and a raging fever, accompanied by a grotesque delirium of some two weeks, had been the result. As the tide of hallucinations had ebbed a half-familiar ghost had stood by my bed. I was aware, as if in a dream, that the phantom in brown was Capt. Dan Chandler, an old friend from home. For days afterward I had struggled with the jigsaw bits of information dropped during his visit. There had been a terrible mixup over my situation, it seemed, and I had been officially reported "killed in action" and "died of wounds" upon various occasions. The few dictated messages I had been able to send home apparently had not relieved the tension there and I understood now that the conflicting statements and jumbled chronology of the official notices and of my infrequent letters had only served to accentuate the uncertainty.

Capt. Chandler had received a cable from my father and had left a nearby post of duty to make a search for me. He hastened to allay their fears by replying in a message saying that I was still above ground.

Now that I was able to take some interest in the curlicued watermarks upon the ceiling over my bed, I had begun to realize that there were absent men and women, who shared everything but the actual physical experience of war with their men who were at the front. I had begun to sense the mental tortures these spiritual camp followers must experience, separated from the combatants as they were by an insurmountable barrier of space.

Six months. How often the lurid kaleidoscope had passed in review upon that ceiling over my head. The fantastic picture unfolded again, induced by one of many recent fits of rummaging through a Red Cross ditty bag, which held all my worldly possessions: Tim's old letter, which had been in the pocket of mine and Stacy's blouse when I had been wounded; a twisted explosive bullet and its jagged contents, which had been removed from my hip piecemeal; a few souvenirs given me by the Boche prisoners that fatal day in the Bois du Jury; a picture of Wally, clipped from a rotogravure page, titled, "killed in action," somewhere along the route of those six months; a batch of mail that had come to hand before several hospital moves had brought complete isolation from the outside world.

How remote, yet how vivid were the events of my active life in France. That bitter winter of 1917, the days of Badonviller and the trenches, the Champagne, the deaths of Tim and Owen, the march to St. Mihiel, even the dreadful ambulance ride from Flirey to Toul on that red-letter day of September 12, seemed equally far away. And that midnight arrival at Toul, which I would never forget. I was lugged into an anaesthetizing room, amid a confusing din of metallic sounds, anxious voices, muffled groans, and those weird sirens that still murmured "good luck" above the buzzing in my head. A nurse entered the small alcove wiping her mouth; through the swinging doors there were glimpses of white-robed figures who seemed to be eating a snack in the operating room, surrounded by the gagging odor of ether and by splattered gore.

The operating room crew would be through eating soon, the nurse announced, as she began to prepare for my entry into the arena of blood.

Eighteen hours with a fractured hip and the excruciating sciatic nerve had taught me all I wished to know about the agonies of movement, no matter how slight, and I pleaded with the nurse and the orderlies to wait until I was under ether before lifting me from the stretcher, which I had ridden ever since the German prisoners had picked me up. This momentary victory won, I all but begged for the suffocating fumes that were to bring precious oblivion after forty-eight hours without sleep or rest.

I thought then that I knew something of the ghastly conflict between torture that forbade sleep and a state of physical and nervous exhaustion that demanded nothing less. But that was before I came to, retching, in that madhouse ward where men gasped, whimpered, suffered, and died around my bed of fiery coals; before those numberless days on a jerking hospital train which carried the tortured salvage to Base No. 46, in central France; before those other operations, those frightful dressings at the hands of Col. Hart; before that pillory of a Balkan frame, with its brutal splint, with its ropes and weights, with its traction tongs, or "ice hooks," whose fiendish tusks pierced the flesh behind the knee and clung to the buried bone; before those endless days of torment and eternal nights of anguish, morphine, and gasping men.

Even then I did not realize that the endless days, the eternal nights, would turn into weeks; weeks when a slamming door was a crashing shell, when Carter on my left was often Wally, when Harrington across the way was sometimes Wheeler and sometimes Wolf, when the booming voice of Col. Hart belonged to Perce. Many were the times when I envied Wally the death which he had gone out to meet without a flinch, but which I was only partially able to comprehend.

Somewhere back there in those fantastic weeks I was approached by a Red Cross worker who had mistaken me for the other Hugh, owing to our identical names. Hugh had been "missing in action" since September 16, I gathered through a half-stupor of drugs, and my aunt and uncle had sent frantic cables for information about him. The Red Cross girl vanished with a promise to have the Paris office send me any news which they might be able to secure from the folks at home.

Somewhere back in that lurid past, more shattered men came into the ward from the Argonne to bring mumbling news of the fighting and incoherent gossip of the Rainbow. The new arrivals added to the horrors of the nights and increased the volume of music in the world outside, which seemed always to be drawn from Chopin, as the unseen processions went out, and from the repertoire of John Philip Sousa, as they came back.

Somewhere back there was that hazy affair called an armistice. Walking patients read the news accounts around an ancient stove. Doctors and nurses, probably out of deference to those for whom there was no armistice, seemed subdued about it all. Or perhaps they celebrated it out of earshot of the wards.

It was in December that my one batch of stale forwarded mail arrived. Bob Carter, with gunshot wounds in the calves of his legs, did all of my reading and writing then. It was he who read those old letters from Dad and answered according to my dictation. It was Bob who, after much evasion and after my insistence, read the messages involving the other Hugh. I asked to see them myself, so singular they were, yet arousing no emotional response from me. Even as I read them nearly four months later the coincidence of dates, names, and contents seemed bizarre:

> Sept. 10, 1918
> Dear Hugh—Received your letter today and it was a pleasure to learn that we gave you such a good time up here. Have delivered your messages to Pat, Maj. Baldwin, Codman and Farnsworth and they all send their best.
> Had a letter from Uncle Tom, which I have just finished answering. We have been working pretty hard lately. Ten enemy planes attacked us when we were up today and four of our men were wounded, but managed to get home okeh. I shot one of the Boches down in flames.

Let's hope you are more fortunate from now on and that you go through the rest of this without a scratch. Luck, old man.   Hugh.

Ninety-sixth Aero Squadron, A.P.O. 703.

And the accompanying dispatch:

From: Home and Communication Section.

To: Lieut. Hugh S. Thompson, One Hundred and Sixty-eighth Infantry, A.E.F. (Base Hospital No. 48).

Subject: Lieut. Hugh S. Thompson, Ninety-sixth Aero Squadron, A.P.O., 703.

In reply to your inquiry concerning your cousin, the above-named officer, we have obtained information from our office in Berne that a letter has been received from Lieut. Codman, dated Rastatt prison camp, Sept. 21, 1918. The letter states that Lieut. Hugh S. Thompson, missing in action since Sept. 16, was brought down in flames.

Home and Communication Section, Bureau Home and Hospital Service.

The days dragged on toward Christmas, after these messages, which left me so strangely immune to their tragic import. The freezing nights were filled with whimpering sounds and with an apparition that now vanished into the wailing shadows and now emerged again to hover around my bed. Sometimes Miss Breen, my night nurse, was June; sometimes she was my mother; while at other times she was just Nora Breen. No one could lift me so carefully as she, no one could so gently tuck the blankets around the ropes and pulleys, the fiendish appurtenances of my Balkan frame. The apparition vanished completely during one of my bad spells, making an unbearable world more unbearable still. I asked for her continually, only to be met by exasperating subterfuge from Miss Pell and Bob, who must have sensed just how essential Nora was. Nurses were decorating the ward with ivy, the day before Christmas, when one of them inadvertently dropped the word that resurrected my conscious emotions from the limbo of forgotten things. Nora Breen had contracted pneumonia in the draughty, freezing ward. Nora Breen had died a week before.

Overwhelming sorrow, a profound sense of loss, welled up, even above the variety of physical torments and the torpor of drugs. What an exacting taskmaster was this thing called war; this way of intense life and sudden death that never permitted things to happen when they took place. Tim and Owen had been killed on the Ourcq and I had heard the tragic news a month late. Hugh had been killed four days after I was wounded and six days after he had written me and the tardy word of his death had left me unbelieving still. Wally and Wheeler, Gilbert and Wolf; Stradikopulos and others had really died in that dripping forest behind Flirey. Later, I had seen some of them lying crumpled in the mud, with my own eyes, yet could not seem to comprehend. How poignantly strange, how overwhelming that they should die that Christmas Eve when the news of Nora's death sank in; that Christmas Eve which brought such vivid memories of another Christmas Eve, only a year ago, but now so far away; that Christmas Eve when the ward was full of men who hung on veritable crosses and the snowy night outside murmured with the carols of those who still knew unblemished faith; that Christmas Eve when a chorus of visiting doctors and nurses stood enveloped before my bed in a nimbus of feeble lamplight, their voices plaintive over that melting but grotesquely inappropriate hymn:

> *Silent night, holy night,*
> *All is calm, all is bright. . . .*

March and April wove themselves into the dragging history of Savenay. Six months turned into eight. A window opposite my bed, framing a patch of blue, peeping tendrils behind the sill, testified that spring was lavishing itself upon the world of Brittany outside.

Nights that were long and wakeful, despite the whisky and aspirin which had been substituted for morphine, ran into lengthy days. Now delicious, now fretful catnaps mingled with

feeble levity and numerous false alarms that the fractured fe-
murs were going home. Arm fractures, amputations, and several emphysema cases were lugged out to hospital trains
which were said to be headed for Brest and St. Nazaire.

Everyone was glad to see Fleming get a break in luck.
Fleming, the half-man, who clung so desperately to his legs,
only to lose them in the end. While he enjoyed a temporary
advantage, now that he was free from the intense agony that
those legs had cost, a man did not need a crystal to see what
life would hold for him.

May crawled along at a snail-like pace. Chance word from
Miss McMahon, one of the day nurses, who had a brother in
the 149th Field Artillery, revealed that even the Rainbow had
long since marched out of Germany and crossed the deep blue
sea. The tardy knowledge left me strangely lonely, despite
transient pals in adjoining bunks.

Days and nights. Nights and days. I continued to consult the
darkness and those educational curlicues overhead while
Douglas, Miller, Bartram, Colley, and I waited for our "ship to
come in." Another rumor was wafted from the world outdoors.
The hospital ship *Mercy* would be docking at St. Nazaire almost any day and we were going home. The news was greeted
with feeble hoots of derision and with the usual parody on
"Smiles":

> *There are ships that tote th' rations,*
> *There are ships that lug th' mail.*
> *There are ships that fetch th' ammunition,*
> *There are ships that rarely ever sail.*
> *There are ships that carry Pres'dent Wilson,*
> *They are mighty giants of th' foam.*
> *But I'll swap 'em all for just a rowboat,*
> *If that rowboat will take me home.*

In spite of the ingrained unbelief, the rumor grew into truth.
A flurry of nurses and doctors, an inspection of casts and
meaningful dressing of wounds, and the pinning of authorita-
tive red tags to our bed jackets, could mean but one thing.

At last we were really going home. What a medley of emotions followed as the astounding fact soaked in. I lay in a trembling hysteria of expectant gladness and poignant reverie
through that last long night. Cigarettes dancing like fireflies in
the darkness of the ward, unseen movements and restless
sighs, indicated that I had wakeful company who shared the
feelings which were overwhelming me.

Home. What an enticing heaven was home. How could it
ever be home without Tim and his galloping laugh; without
Wally and his serious eyes, his whimsical grin; without Nora
Breen, whose caressing voice and gentle hands also beckoned
me to stay? Home. How would I ever manage to become ad-
justed to June and Dad and all of those other strange folks? If
what the doctors said were true, I would have ample time to
answer questions such as these. After all there were those
operations ahead; home, for months to come, could only mean
a hospital in some unnamed corner of the United States. After
all, there would be more wakeful nights, more ceilings upon
which to stare and think. But how much I had already learned
from the ceiling, which I was now to leave and how much
those curlicues had taught me that I did not wish to know.

Yes I was going home, but some of me, much of me, was
buried in France, I knew. I knew, too, that things could never
be the same again, for war, like some sadistic Frankenstein,
vivisected a man, as if to see what made him tick and then
failed to put all of the pieces back.

War stripped a man of his protective illusions and left only
a terrible wisdom, which he had neither wanted nor con-
sciously sought. War made a man suffer the tortures of the
flesh and of the mind and spirit, which were matters of even
greater import. Above all else, war meant separation. War
meant separation from a prosaic past that, by no stretch of the
imagination could be shed lightly and then pulled on again
like a comfortable old shoe. War meant separation from the
present and from an immediate future that would not wait on
exiled men. War added people like Tim, Wally, Owen, and
Nora Breen to the list of a man's necessities and then snatched
these essentials right out of his life, when he seemed to need

them most. War separated a man from the living as well as from the dead. Even the Rainbow would dissolve, perhaps already had dissolved, and its human remnants scattered to the winds. John and Perce, if they still lived; McDonough, Stryker, and Jim, the survivors of my old platoon; all of these had gone into an exasperating void that sent no tangible echoes across the leagues of geography and space. I would rarely, if ever, see any of these priceless friends again. I had joined the Rainbow and found these men. I had followed the Rainbow through hell, drawn irresistibly by the comradeships that such men gave. I had followed the Rainbow around the world only, it seemed, to lose these fierce attachments, which could never be replaced. And now, from this new day, whose first gray shafts of light crept through the windows, I must follow the Rainbow out into boundless time.

Notes

Chapter One. On the Way

1. The "ninety days" refers to the three months deemed necessary by the U.S. Army to prepare a second lieutenant. Such officers were known as "ninety-day wonders." Thompson had been stationed at Camp Mills, Mineola, New York.

2. In 1914, at the beginning of the war, American engineer Herbert Hoover, living in London, was asked by the U.S. Embassy to head a committee to assist some 120,000 stranded American travelers in getting home. Subsequently, Hoover focused his humanitarian efforts to help the starving people of Belgium, which had been occupied by the Germans. Hoover initiated the Commission Relief in Belgium, which found financing for food to feed eleven million people in Belgium and northern France.

   The white banner "Belgium Relief," on the sides of the ships carrying the food, was to guarantee secure passage for the transports.

3. During the period of American neutrality, 1914–17, President Woodrow Wilson on one occasion said that "There is such a thing as a man being too proud to fight."

4. The zeppelins were long, cylindrical-bodied German airships, designed by Count Ferdinand von Zeppelin.

5. The British "Tommys," named for the fictitious "Tommy Atkins," is the equivalent of the American "John Doe." The name may have originated in 1815 War Office publications that showed how a Soldier's Book should be filled out. "Private Tommy Atkins" was the sample name used. Blighty is British slang for England, or home.

6. Gobs, in British slang, are sailors.

7. WAACs were members of the Women's Army Auxiliary Corps. A "poilu," in World War I slang, is a French front-line soldier.

8. Because of censorship, locations and addresses became "somewhere in France."

9. "Madelon," the French soldier's song, and "Over There," the Americans' song.

10. The French Chasseurs were mounted troops (cavalry).

11. Confiture is any kind of French confection.

12. A Chauchat was a light machine gun. A trench mortar could be fired from within the trench.

13. Estaminet is a small French café.
14. Old-timers were the officers and men of the Regular Army, as compared to the "new" wartime draftees and enlistees.
15. A "looey" is a lieutenant.
16. "Gare": The railway station, at Lyons.

Chapter Two. Somewhere in France

1. The 42nd Division took heavy casualties, as did all of the veteran divisions, and in the Meuse-Argonne casualties rose above 5,000. The ratio of killed to wounded was 1 to 4 or 1 to 5. Second lieutenants suffered more casualties than other officers, and by the end of the war the American Expeditionary Forces faced an acute lack of lieutenants in the companies and platoons.
2. Camion is French for a lorry or truck.
3. An Annamite is a native of Annam, a region of French Indo-China, in east-central Vietnam.
4. The Sam Browne belt was worn by officers of the AEF. General Pershing had admired its use in the British army, where it had been adapted from the Indian army. The belt offered a tailored look and called attention to its wearer as being an officer.
5. In World War I the U.S. infantryman was called a doughboy, though the word is said to have been part of Army slang for many years.
6. 40 Hommes–8 Chevaux: A boxcar capable of holding either forty men or eight horses.
7. Hardtack was a small biscuit (often of saltine-cracker size), or bread, made only with flour and water. It was a naval and military food staple as it "traveled" well. "Goldfish" were sardines.
8. K.P., kitchen police. The word "police" meant work of any sort.

Chapter Three. Rimaucourt

1. Billeting for officers and men was, respectively, rooms in villages or barns and stables.
2. Regular Army officers were condescending and often hostile to reservists, no doubt considering them not as capable as Regulars.
3. Thompson was a lieutenant of a platoon of fifty men.
4. AWOL, of course, is absent without leave; MP, Military Police.
5. A then popular knife.
6. Issoudun was an aviation instruction center made up of twelve airfields, an intermediate quartermaster depot, an armament storage depot, and a prisoner of war enclosure.
7. "Bon chance": good luck!

Chapter Four. The Raid

1. Slum was army stew, known also as slumgullion.
2. In 1916, President Wilson had sent the National Guard to the Mexican border, following Mexican leader Pancho Villa's raid into the town of Columbus, New Mexico, in which seventeen Americans were killed. The then Brigadier General Pershing took 6,000 Regulars across the border to hunt Villa.
3. Major General Hunter Liggett was about to become a corps commander. In the midst of the battle of the Meuse-Argonne he took command of First Army, with Pershing becoming an Army group commander.
4. The "square" organization of U.S. divisions in World War I allowed for two infantry brigades and an artillery brigade. The infantry brigades each had two regiments, each of the latter three battalions, which in turn contained four companies of 250 men. Brigades had brigadier generals, regiment colonels, battalion majors, company captains, and platoon lieutenants or (if there were insufficient lieutenants) sergeants. U.S. divisions were twice the size of British, French, and German divisions. Pershing believed their size allowed for staying power; critics maintained that the divisions were too large to command.
5. The Lorraine Cross is a double-barred cross whose history goes back to at least 800 A.D., when it was used by Christians in the Orient. Essentially a symbol of peace, it was familiar to all.
6. Army drills were close order and extended order, the former for parades and marching through streets, the latter for attack, with men dispersed.
7. What the men called "g.u. stations" were no doubt "genital-urinary" medical aid stations/facilities, set up for venereal disease treatment. Troops were regularly "inspected" for the disease, often on a weekly basis.
8. The Stokes mortar, designed by the Briton F. W. C. Stokes, had a three-inch cast-iron "bomb." The mortar could fire up to twenty-two bombs per minute, with a range of 1,200 yards. It became the standard issue for the British army and was the most widely used mortar by the Allies.

Chapter Five. The Trenches

1. The "77s" were German light artillery pieces.
2. "Pioneers" were the labor troops that built roads and dug trenches.
3. Duckboards were strips of wood laid over the muddy floor of a trench.

4. A salient is a part of a battle line that projects pointedly into opposing territory.
5. Six- and three-star rocket signals burst into six and three stars, respectively, when fired. "No man's land" was the strip of land between opposing front lines. In World War I, on the Western Front, this strip might range from a few yards wide to several hundred.
6. Bully beef was canned or pickled beef (probably evolving from the French "bouillir," to boil). Bully beef and hardtack were often called "iron rations."
7. "Boche!" . . . "Pas Boche!": "Germans!" . . . "Not Germans!"
8. To "stand to" meant the troops in the front line manned the fire step (the firing position in their trench), alert for enemy attack.
9. Reference is to the 75mm French light artillery piece provided the U.S Army. In the three-regiment artillery brigade of American divisions, one had 155mm guns, also of French manufacture.

Chapter Six. More of Same

1. The parapet was a mound of earth, or stone, along the front of the trench, to protect the troops.
2. The Maxim machine gun was developed by the American-born inventor Hiram Maxim, who had moved to London. The Maxim could fire 500–600 rounds per minute. The British army adopted the weapon in 1889.
3. "Qui vive": on the alert.
4. A sap was a trench or tunnel, extending out from other trenches in "no man's land," used as a listening/observation post.
5. Baylor was a preparatory school, not yet a university. Thompson thereafter spent two years at The Citadel.
6. A whiz-bang was the German high-velocity shell, fired from an Austrian-made artillery piece; it came over so fast that it struck earth, or whatever else, before it could be heard.
7. Shells sounded like express trains.
8. A parados was an elevation of earth (a mound along the back of a trench), to prevent attack from the rear.
9. Each soldier was issued a shelter half—half of a small tent, which when joined with another formed a shelter.
10. Frenchmen were called Frogs because they ate frogs' legs.
11. "Americans good! The war, not good!"

Chapter Seven. To Bru and Back

1. The Y.M.C.A. (Young Men's Christian Association) had some 13,000 men and women workers serving the AEF. The Y.M.C.A. was founded in England in 1844; it came to the United States and Canada by 1851.
2. The Croix de Guerre ("cross of war") was awarded to French officers and enlisted men for bravery in battle.
3. The weekly *Stars and Stripes* was the AEF newspaper, written and published by men from the ranks. The first edition came out on February 8, 1918, in Paris, and it eventually had a circulation of over 500,000.
4. "Caught in the 'breeze,'" suggested someone caught up in the prevailing winds of current events.
5. It was a time of danger for the Allied cause, as the Bolshevik Revolution had resulted in Russia's withdrawal from the war and allowed the transfer of German divisions to the Western Front. The High Command on November 11, 1917, made the decision to open a gigantic offensive. The first blow was against the British Fifth Army, holding the line between the British sector and that of the French. Beginning March 21, this assault nearly broke up the Fifth Army, for the Germans drove back the line fifty kilometers and took 80,000 prisoners. The second assault opened on April 9, a third May 27, a fourth June 8, and the fifth and last on July 15. Thompson heard the rumor of the opening of the second, which for the British army proved not as difficult to contain as the first.
6. A "sulphur dial" was a wristwatch whose dial was composed of sulphur, perhaps amongst other elements, typical of the manufacture of the time, and the numerals glowed in the dark.
7. "Cits" was slang for "civilian/citizen clothes."

Chapter Eight. Badonviller

1. Field Marshal Paul von Hindenburg was the commander of the German Eastern Army, later Chief of General Staff of the German Field Army, and in 1925 elected Chancellor of the new Weimar Republic. Kaiser Wilhelm II, the German emperor during World War I, was considered ill-prepared for his position.
2. "Tronche," in French, literally means a "mug" or "face," referring disparagingly to the Germans.
3. The sausage-shaped balloons were used by the Germans as observation posts, as well as for aerial barriers with cables strung between balloons to impede Allied aircraft.
4. "Read shirts" referred to searching for lice, so-called cooties.
5. J. Pierpont Morgan, American financier, had headed the banking

company J. P. Morgan, which was involved with the financing of World War I; William G. McAdoo was Secretary of the Treasury under President Woodrow Wilson; and financier Bernard Baruch was chairman of the War Industries Board.

Chapter Nine. The Last Trench Days

1. Enfilade fire, also called "flanking fire," is firing in the direction of the length of a trench, line, or troop column.

Chapter Ten: Paradise

1. Y.M.C.A. buildings were known as huts.
2. Lauder was the well-known music hall humorist, a Scot who appeared with kilts and a pipe.
3. *Chattanooga Times.*

Chapter Eleven. Hospital and Home

1. Apparently first employed in the Balkan countries, such a splint or frame provided overhead bars and pulleys for suspension, traction, and counter-traction.
2. On May 27, 1918, the German Army attacked along the Chemin des Dames, a sector commanded by a French general who despite warning had bunched his men in the front lines. Casualties were heavy.
3. Lieut. Col. William J. Donovan was a New York lawyer who had been a member of the "Fighting 69th," the city's National Guard unit. Father Francis P. Duffy was regimental chaplain.
4. The U.S. Army in World War I perpetuated a theory in organization of divisions that designated the first ten as Regular Army (for that reason the numbers were spelled out). Divisions in the twenties, thirties, and forties were National Guard (numbers in arabic); seventies, eighties, and nineties were National Army, draftees. The trouble with the nomenclature was that Regular troops could not fill the first divisions, nor could the Guard those designated for them. In April 1917, the Regular Army mustered 130,000 men and officers, the Guard 180,000. During the war the strength of the army rose to 3.8 million.
5. The 41st was a replacement division; hence the campaign hats.
6. Joyce Kilmer, the poet, was killed while with the Rainbow.

Chapter Twelve. Wounded Again

1. Massing of German troops in the salient that included Soissons, captured at the time of the Chemin des Dames, was a sign of a new of-

fensive, which came on July 15. The French learned of its immi-
nence and hence the preparation.

2. It was true. The opening barrage for this fifth and last great German
attack on July 15 had been fearful, but the offensive quickly failed.
Losses on the German side from all of the offensives were equal to
those of the Allies, 350,000 killed and wounded.

Chapter Thirteen. Recovery

1. "It is sad. It is a pity. So young, so young."
2. The first full-length moving picture (1915).
3. St. Mihiel had been a German salient since 1914.
4. At the time of Belleau Wood, late May 1918, a censor had passed a
reference to the Marines in someone's letter home, which had identified where they were, for in the AEF there was a single Marine brigade, in the Second Division.

Chapter Fourteen. Home Again

1. The Lafayette Escadrille was a group of Americans who volunteered
to be aviators for the French prior to the American declaration of
war.
2. Youngest son of former President Theodore Roosevelt.
3. Major General Frank T. Menoher commanded the division.
4. When the war began the U.S. Army was relying on the Springfield
.03, the best infantry rifle in the world. However, although 600,000
had been manufactured in the Springfield arsenal, they could not be
produced as rapidly as needed. The resort was to the British Enfield,
already in production in the United States, modified to take Springfield cartridges and known as the Lee-Enfield.

Chapter Fifteen. Preparation

1. These "iron animals" were the French light Renault tanks. In battle
they were less fearsome than they appeared, lacking armor, slow
(five or six miles per hour), and vulnerable to artillery, ditches, and
shell holes. Mechanically unreliable, they suffered innumerable
breakdowns. They were difficult for crews, with little protection
against jolts and bumps; they smelled of oil and gasoline; inside tem-
peratures rose to 130 degrees and higher.
2. The Hindenburg Line was originally the name given to the strong
defensive position held by the Germans between Soissons and
Cambrai in 1917; later the Allies applied the name to strong German
positions on other parts of the front.

Chapter Sixteen. St. Mihiel

1. Minenwerfer were small German mortars.
2. For most of the troops, St. Mihiel was an easy victory, a battle that was over in a day, although it did stretch on for three more days nominally until there was no more danger of a counterattack. The Germans were pulling out of the salient when the battle opened. This proved part of their undoing, for the trains were on the roads when the American artillery opened and concentrated on the roads, not at first realizing how good the targets were. It was said by waggish observers that St. Mihiel was the battle in which the Americans relieved the Germans. But for Thompson and others in the 42nd Division, the battle was no joke.

Further Reading

The 42nd Division's constituency, the source of its personnel, was widespread, and perhaps that is most of the reason why the division inspired so many books. It may also have been the division's popular name—the Rainbow. A lesser reason for the books was the "Fighting 69th," the New York City regiment of the National Guard, which became the 165th Infantry, filled with well-known city figures who, if not celebrating the division, were celebrating the regiment that in its traditions reached back before the Civil War.

It was understandable that every regiment in the 42nd Division, including the artillery regiments, enjoyed recitals of war service in book form. The 165th, the New Yorkers' own, had a notable account by its chaplain, Father Francis P. Duffy, *Father Duffy's Story: A Tale of Humor and Heroism, of Life and Death with the Fighting Sixty-Ninth* (Garden City, N.Y., 1919). For the 166th Infantry Regiment there is R. M. Cheseldine, *Ohio in the Rainbow: Official Story of the 166th Infantry, 42nd Division, in the World War* (Columbus: Heer, 1924). The 167th is in William H. Amerine, *Alabama's Own in France* (New York: Eaton and Gettinger, 1919); the 168th in John H. Taber, *The Story of the 168th Infantry*, 2 vols. (Iowa City: Iowa State Historical Society, 1925). The 149th Field Artillery Regiment is in Charles G. MacArthur, *A Bug's Eye View of the War* (n.p., 1919), republished as *War Bugs* (Garden City, N.Y.: Doubleday, Doran, 1929). For the 150th Regiment see Elmer W. Sherwood's memoir, *Rainbow Hoosier* (Indianapolis, 1919), and its forthcoming revision with the title of *A Soldier in World War I*, Robert H. Ferrell, ed. (Indianapolis: Indiana Historical Society, 2004). The 151st Regiment is best seen in the diary of its colonel, George E. Leach, published privately in 1923, reprinted as *War Diary* (Roanoke, Va.: Rainbow Division Veterans, 1962).

A remarkable volume on the Rainbow Division is by the 149th Field Artillery Regiment colonel who replaced General

Michael J. Lenihan as brigade commander in mid-October 1918, Henry J. Reilly, *Americans All, The Rainbow at War: Official History of the 42nd Rainbow Division in the War* (Columbus: Heer, 1936). General Reilly gathered everything he could find about the Rainbow, including individual testimonies (sometimes edited a bit).

Beyond the above titles are perhaps thirty or forty more, by participants and admirers, the majority worth reading. The most recent is James J. Cooke, *The Rainbow Division in the Great War* (Westport, Conn.: Praeger, 1994).

For manuscript collections, the best resource is the U.S. Army Military History Institute, a part of the Army War College at Carlisle Barracks, Carlisle, Pennsylvania. Beginning in the 1970s, the Army sent thousands of questionnaires to World War I veterans to survey their service; the questionnaires brought in letters, diaries, and memoirs, all now gathered by divisions. In addition, the Carlisle Barracks records hold a long-maintained name file.

The National Archives, with its collections in a new building in College Park, Maryland, possesses an enormous mass of official records bearing on the war, including papers of divisions, of which the 42nd's holdings number several dozen boxes—perhaps fifteen feet of field orders, reports, and summaries of action.

Index

ISBN 1-58544-290-9

90000